What Every Christian Author Needs to Know

Activate Your Scribe Anointing

By Best-Selling Author
Jennifer LeClaire

Published by Awakening Media
P.O. Box 30563
Fort Lauderdale, Fla. 33301
www.awakeningmedia.com

Printed in the United States of America

Unless otherwise noted, Scripture is taken from the Modern English Version of the Bible.

ACKNOWLEDGMENTS

I'm grateful for the giants in the publishing industry that have taught me so well what it takes to succeed in the industry, from Tessie DeVore, former publisher at Charisma House, to Larry Sparks, publisher of Destiny Image, to Jane Campbell, editorial director at Chosen Books, to Joel Kneedler, Publisher of Harper Collins' Emanate Books. I'm also grateful to the many editors I've worked with over the years in these organizations and earlier in my career as a journalist. At some level, writing really is a team sport.

ENDORSEMENT

Jennifer LeClaire has an anointing and authority to write about writing. The anointing is the supernatural power of the Holy Spirit influencing what she writes, but the authority is demonstrated in how she writes. The content comes from Heaven, but the delivery is something that Jennifer has discovered over years.

The best teachers are not theorists; they are the practitioners. This book is a treasure, as it comes from someone who has practiced the principles she is sharing—to some amazing, breakthrough results. Furthermore, this book will activate you to get started on your own personal writing journey.

In fact, I believe it just might offer the missing "next step" for those of you who have *not* written anything yet, and for those of you who are in the process of developing a manuscript.

Larry Sparks
Publisher, Destiny Image
Author of *Breakthrough Faith,* co-author of *The Fire That Never Sleeps* and *Arise*

TABLE OF CONTENTS

INTRODUCTION

If you picked up this book, you have an absolute passion to write words that impact the masses—or at least a curious desire to explore the world of wordsmithing, scribing, chronicling or one of the myriad writing expressions that make up this creative craft. You probably have a God-given gift and a deep desire that that gift will one day make room for you with readers searching for material in your genre.

Well, my friend, I have good news for you. Proverbs 18:16—"A man's gift makes room for him, and brings him before great men"—is true. If you release your gift with passion (and skill), it will carry your voice to places you never thought you could go. Indeed, your words could inspire the hearts of great men and women for ages to come long after you've gone home to be with the Lord.

I am living proof. When I was five years old, my kindergarten teacher assigned us to create a small book, complete with a story, artwork, and bound cover. It was quite a task for a five-year-old but I took it on with zeal. My story was about a little girl and boy who set their hearts to rocket to the moon in a spaceship—and succeeded! (Seems I was always a dreamer.)

During a parent-teacher conference, my kindergarten teacher, Ms. Greene, prophesied to my mother concerning my future. Well, she may not have known she was prophesying but she absolutely was. She told my mother I would most definitely become a writer when I grew up.

Of course, the enemy fought against that impromptu prophecy tooth and nail. I always loved reading—perhaps because as a child I was laid up in the hospital and later confined to bed in a full body cast twice. I didn't have much else to do but read, draw and watch *I Love Lucy*. But the enemy's injurious attack turned into a blessing, according to Romans 8:28. I read several books a week throughout my childhood and even into my teenage years. I developed a love for reading and learning.

But I still didn't like writing.

In fact, I hated writing.

I was in advanced English classes throughout high school. I clearly had communication giftings and aptitudes. But I hated writing so much that I would wait until after a term paper was due to start it and only then completed it to avoid failing the class. I always turned in my writing assignments late and took two downgrades as a penalty. Even still—even with a rushed presentation—I would have received an A if I had turned it in on time. Writing just didn't interest me. I wanted to be a psychologist.

When I got to college, I decided to join the school newspaper. Mind you, I still had no ambition to write news stories but thought of it as a social opportunity to meet people in a new city. However, I soon discovered I was good at writing. I enjoyed writing. I developed a passion for writing. Soon, I rose to assistant news editor, then news editor, then features editor, and then managing editor of the college paper. I wrote with various pseudonyms because there was never enough content to fill the pages. I did it all, from A to Z. And my boyfriend was the chief photographer, so we made a great team.

My ambitions shifted. I still didn't want to be a writer, per se, but I no longer wanted to be a psychologist. Instead, I wanted to be a filmmaker. My burning desire to write and edit for the silver screen opened me up to an entirely different genre that took my creativity to new heights. I never officially entered the film world professionally due to a horrible car accident that took me off track, but I did have professional screenwriting consultants coach me on how to write two scripts—one short film and one full-length movie.

Over the years, I've successfully shifted through many career crossovers, as I call them. Beyond journalism and film screenwriting, I've written magazine articles, billboard advertisements, marketing copy for Fortune 500 firms, TV commercial scripts, press releases, brochures, website copy, technical manuals, technology books, real estate books, Christian books, and more. I've severed as a project manager, editor, and ghostwriter. As I often say, if it can be written, I've probably written it.

Guess what? You can too. I crossed over many times in my career—not because I wanted to be a generalist or a Jack of all Trades, per se. I crossed over because I wanted to explore different expressions of my gift and voice. It was challenging. It was fun. Maybe you are more of a generalist than a true in-depth expert in your field. That's great! Do what God has called you to do. Do what you love. Live your passion.

If you want to take your writing—any kind of writing—to the next level, this book is for you. The pages herein offer a strategic starting point to share with you everything a Christian writer needs to know.

But don't let the title fool you. This is not just for Christian writers. I was raised up as a media voice in the secular world. That's where I learned almost everything I know about the principles of solid writing. The difference now is that I am no longer writing for *The New York Times* or Associated Press. I'm writing for the Lord. Whether you are a seasoned professional or just getting started, you and your readers will benefit from you reading—and applying—what you learn in the pages of this book.

You may want to consider joining my Writers Network. You can find that online at www.writenow.network. I have created seminars and webinars for writers. You can find those at www.schoolofthespirit.tv. I pray this book gives you the answers you need—and elicits more questions! Obviously, I can't cover everything in a single book, but you will find a wealth of information in the pages ahead. Happy writing!

Chapter 1
Where in the World Do I Start?

I started my career writing for free in the 1990s. Yes, free. A young entrepreneurial-minded man in India launched an online magazine and was looking for contributors. Keep in mind this was still the early days of the Internet. This forward-thinking content entrepreneur was carving a niche for himself on the World Wide Web.

Although I never saw a dime for the work, this was a strategic investment in my early career. Penning online articles per gratis forced me into the habit of writing—and rewriting. It helped me develop discipline and offered me an opportunity to grow in my gifts. Sure, I could have rolled out my own blog. But in those days, it wasn't as easy as it is now. Wordpress was still years away from hitting the scene. It was a different world and I was new at it. I decided to pay my ducs—to sow into another man's work. That's never a bad idea when you are working to penetrate a new market.

Soon, I got what I felt was a huge breakthrough (in those days it was). I got a steady gig writing for *American Window Cleaner Magazine* ... I got paid a whopping four cents a word to write about something I knew absolutely nothing about. But I wasn't in it for the money. I was in it for the experience. I also wrote for local parenting magazines and took any other opportunity I could find, free or paid. I queried anybody and everybody waiting for my bigger breakthrough. And it came!

As the Bible says, when you are faithful over a little, God will make you ruler over much (see Matthew 25:23). After sowing into the young Indian man's blog and being willing to work for pennies in an industry magazine that made me yawn, suddenly a former editor of the college newspaper on which I served contacted me about a freelance opportunity with an online magazine at which he was working. And I actually got paid!

Unfortunately, that magazine soon went bust—but I left an impression. The creators of that business magazine got a huge contract with a Fortune 500 company that wanted to launch a website for small business owners. Because they liked my work, they gave me an opportunity to be part of the launch team. Soon, I was cranking out 10 stories a day and making a significant freelance wage. And when the project manager went out on maternity leave indefinitely during a growth spurt, they hired me and another freelancer to serve as project managers supervising about 10 writers each.

Then it happened. The dot-com bubble burst and the site went belly up. The big breakthrough became a massive bust. I had all my eggs in this single basket and I lost everything. Around the same time, my husband abandoned me and my then-two-year-old daughter. And shortly after that I was falsely accused of a crime I did not commit and landed in jail. The prosecutors threatened a five-year prison sentence. I had hit rock bottom. Thank God the evangelists came through the county jail preaching the gospel. I surrendered my heart to the Lord and everything changed.

Of course, I was broke and in debt financially but wealthy and free spiritually. The charges against me were ruled a gross error of justice, but I knew the Justifier. I was husbandless. I was jobless. I was apartmentless. I was dogless. I was carless. But I was looking at things from a whole new perspective. I wasn't chasing success anymore. I was chasing Jesus.

When I got born again, all I wanted to do was write for the Lord. That didn't happen overnight, despite my best efforts and strong desires.

I tried to get a writing gig with every Christian magazine in the world, but I didn't have enough knowledge of the Word of God to qualify. So, I continued to work for Fortune 500 companies, like Microsoft, Amazon, Yahoo, IBM, CBS,

Intercontinental Hotel, NetSuite, Pitney Bowes, MasterCard, Hyatt Hotels, and Ryder. No, my writing break in the Christian world didn't happen overnight—because I didn't have anything to say. I didn't have any Word in me. I wasn't familiar with the ways of God. I didn't have a prophetic perspective on life.

I studied, prayed, and pressed. (Let this be a lesson to you in whatever field you are hoping to catch a break.) Within two years, I was named editor of an international Christian magazine. I interviewed the likes of Reinhard Bonnke, Joyce Meyer, Myles Munroe, and many other Christian leaders, and started penning a column on the prophetic. Two years later, those columns served as the baseline for my first book, *The Heart of the Prophetic*. Major leaders in the prophetic movement endorsed that book. I was shocked. Clearly, the hand of the Lord was on my life to publish God's truths.

Some years later, I started freelancing for *Charisma* magazine. Soon enough, they brought me on as news editor, the online managing editor, and finally senior editor. I became the first female in the magazine's 40-plus year history to assume the editor-in-chief role. I've also written over 25 books—both secular and Christian—and been published in some of the most recognized newspapers and magazines in the world, including *The New York Times*, *The Christian Science Monitor*, *Architectural Digest*, *Men's Health*, *Miami Herald*, and *Inc.*

My writing has reached every nation of the earth and I've had best-selling books and massively viral articles and podcasts. It's a jaw-dropping blessing after a series of earth-shattering experiences. I give God all the glory.

I still remember the many rejection letters I received before I got to where I am today. Those stung! I still remember the thrill of getting published for the first time—a short story I wrote based on my experiences in Cuba appeared in *The New York Times* best-selling book, *Chicken Soup for the Woman's Soul*. I jumped up and down for a while and called everyone I knew. I still remember when I got my first contract with a book publisher after self-publishing six of my own books. That was even more thrilling.

The point of my sharing my personal journey with you is this: Everybody starts somewhere on the path to become a successful writer. You may have already started a few times and given up a few times. Maybe you are ready to start again. Maybe you have a great idea and need some motivation to get it off the ground. Or maybe you want to write and you have no clue where to start.

In this chapter, you'll discover some strategies for finding subject matter that you're passionate about—and subject matter that will resonate with your target audience.

What on Earth Am I Going to Write About?

Maybe you've already started writing the next great American novel, life-changing children's book, marketing copy for a Fortune 500 company, epic screenplay, or transformational weekly blogs. Or maybe you aren't quite sure where to begin. Or, then again, maybe you've started three books, 10 blogs, and 50 poems but rarely finish a piece of work.

If you are struggling for the next great idea—if you spend more time than you know you should staring at a computer screen asking yourself, "What on earth am I going to write about?"—then you need to shift your mindset. Indeed, it's possible that while you are trying to work up the next winning idea, you are working yourself out of your creativity.

Consider the words of George Orwell, author of the classic books *1984* and *Animal Farm*, who once said: "When I sit down to write a book, I do not say to myself, 'I am going to produce a work of art.' I write it because there is some lie that I want to expose, some fact to which I want to draw attention, and my initial concern is to get a hearing."

If you are reading this book, you aren't writing for your own reading enjoyment. You want other people to read what you write. You want to make an impact on the lives of your readers. You understand the power that lies in the written word—a medium God used to share with us His ways, His will and His good news of salvation. You want to inform, entertain, educate, or persuade people with the words that roll off the tip of your pen—or your computer keyboard. But even with a burning desire in your heart to write, it can be difficult to settle on a topic. It can be challenging to determine what you are going to write about.

Still, you can't just sit around and wait for inspiration to come to you. You have to feed the muse. In other words, you have to give your mind something to think about. There's no lack of relevant subject matter around you. Maybe, like Orwell, it is a lie you want to expose or a fact to which you want to draw attention.

Always remember, curiosity begets creativity. If you are observant to the natural world around you while maintaining sensitivity to the Spirit of God, you will find interesting things to write about in the grocery store, on chance encounters in an elevator, in the workplace, and even in the shower. (I don't know why God wants to talk to me in the shower. I can't carry my notepad in there without getting it wet.) There are characters all around us. Add a little creativity to everyday events and you have a great story plot, life lesson, lie to expose, or encouragement to share.

15 Tips to Feed Your Muse

Luke was a physician who accompanied Paul on his missionary journeys and penned both the Book of Luke and the Book of Acts by the inspiration of the Holy Spirit. We can take some cues from Luke in his chronicling adventures, as well as the Old Testament prophets. I've thrown in a few of my own for good measure.

1. What is God saying right now?

Luke was careful to record what God said—so should you. In Luke 1:13, he recorded Zechariah's supernatural encounter with an angel and the prophetic message about John the Baptist's birth. In Luke 1:26, he recorded Mary's supernatural encounter with an angel who announced the Messiah's through her. Fast forward to Luke 1:67 and we see Zachariah prophesying the coming Messiah.

Read the Book of Luke and the Book of Acts and you'll see clear examples of how Luke consistently chronicled what the Lord was saying and doing. If you aren't already, keep a journal to chronicle what the Lord is saying and doing in and around you, whether through His still small voice, a supernatural encounter, a dream or vision, a revelation from Scripture, prophetic insight into current events, or a prophecy you receive.

2. Pay attention to news headlines.

Although most modern-day news channels are admittedly dark, paying attention to news headlines helps you stay abreast of current events in the world around you. No matter what kind of writing you do, this is vital to your perspective. As a writer, you need to be informed before you can educate or persuade.

You need to know what is happening around you before you can discern what, if anything, the Lord would have you share about current events. You need to understand societal trends if you are going to sound the alarm.

Again, no matter what kind of writing you do, the daily news can inspire you. Visiting Google News once or twice a day is a strategic way to get a rundown on current headlines in many sectors of society around the world. If something strikes your heart, ask the Lord what He is saying in it. Then write down what He shows you. He may give you a prophetic word to release in a blog, or even a book idea. But, again, it all starts with awareness.

3. Comprehend significant events and turning points.
Luke chronicled the changing of the guard from the old to the new covenant. That's why He started his account well before the other four Gospel writers. Luke introduced his Gospel with the birth of John the Baptist because, as a chronicler being led by the Spirit of God, he perceived the significance of this turning point in history and the need to explain it. Readers needed the backstory to better understand the turning point.

Turning points in your life, in the Church, or in society can be fodder for your writing. When the Supreme Court legalized gay marriage, I took that as an opportunity to share what the Lord was saying to America. When tragedies strike, there's an opportunity to speak Holy Spirit-inspired words of comfort. When revival hits a region, there's a chance to noise abroad the power of Jesus.

4. Look for life lessons in spiritual battles.
While Old Testament prophets chronicled natural wars, New Testament chroniclers should be documenting significant spiritual wars in their lives, in their church, in their cities, or around the world—even if those wars manifest in the natural. If you ever plan to write a book, these documented facts will be necessary to support and illustrate the revelation you are bringing forth. Without these real-life examples, books are boring.

When you are battling your way through spiritual warfare—or making intercessory warfare for someone or something else—chronicle your thoughts, what the Lord is saying, the lessons you are learning, and even your emotions.

Here's a wise word of warning: Wait until you are standing in a place of victory before you release any writing about your struggles publicly. Spiritual battles are rich with drama, wisdom principles, and victory tactics that inspire others walking through warfare, but if you want to inspire someone you need to do more than tell about the warfare—you need to offer victory principles that worked for you.

5. Spot societal and spiritual trends.

What positive or negative trends are happening in the world? What about spiritual trends? This ties into keeping abreast of the news while keeping a listening ear to the Spirit. Trends of opioid addiction or pastors falling into scandals could spark in you a Spirit-inspired idea to address solutions to these problems that help the masses. The key is not to offer your opinion, but to offer spiritual insight from the Lord.

6. Become a voice for the concerns of people.

Concerns in society, like racism or the economy or healthcare, could inform your writing. The same holds true regarding concerns, challenges, and problems in the Church, like leadership or finances or today's youth leaving in droves. If people are concerned about a topic, then you have an audience with them. If the Holy Spirit pricks your heart, it becomes your job to dig for the revelation and the solutions that will make your writing relevant.

7. Read your Bible.

This should go without saying, but it needs to be said and bears repeating repeatedly. Reading your Bible—the inspired Word of God—can inspire new revelations for teaching articles, blogs, books, screenplays, poetry, and anything else you feel called to write. The Holy Spirit inspired Scripture and He can inspire you through Scripture.

8. Read through old journals.
If you keep a journal, read through entries from years ago. You may have forgotten some of the battles, victories, prophetic words, and spiritual experiences in your life. The Lord could use stories from those journals to encourage and educate others in their life struggles.

9. Put on some music.
Sometimes, music can inspire our hearts and settle our souls. When I was in high school, the creative writing teacher offered us one-liners from songs and challenged us to write for fifteen minutes based on that single verse. You can do the same thing with your favorite worship song. Who knows where that will take you? Even if you don't do anything with what you wrote, you got your creative writing juices flowing.

10. Go people watching.
I love to people watch. Go sit in a mall or coffee shop and watch people go in and out, around, and about. Listen to their conversations (not in a creepy way!). Observe their body language. This is an especially strategic exercise for fiction writers working to develop compelling, realistic characters.

11. Get outside!
Go for a walk. Explore nature. Get some fresh air. For the better part of 20 years, I lived on the beach. I had

a habit of walking to the ocean, even if just for a few minutes, to get a new perspective. Sometimes getting inspired with a new idea is merely a matter of changing our scenery.

12. Explore quotes from historical and modern figures.

Sites like BrainyQuote.com have a cadre of quotes from historical and modern figures on just about every topic you can imagine. You may strongly disagree with a quip or quote you stumble on while browsing these sites. Perfect! Write a counter quote or an entire argument and use it to populate your blog. On the other hand, you may wholeheartedly agree with what you read and get inspired to expound on a classic quote with some new wisdom for a modern generation.

13. Reduce your stress levels.

If you're stressed out all the time, take a deep breath. Stress kills your creativity. Study after study shows this. Make some time to relax, take a break, exercise, unplug, sleep. Do what you enjoy. Destress and your creativity will rise.

14. Rely on all five senses.

As prophetic people, we have spiritual senses and natural senses. Hyperfocus on the sights, sounds, smells, tastes, and sensations around you—or introduce them into your world. I like the smell of cinnamon and lavender. I diffuse oils when I write. I enjoy the sound of rain, lightning, and thunder. I play rainymood.com when I write as white noise to cut out the distractions. I love the sound of worship. I let that take me into the Spirit. I like the taste of coffee. You get the picture.

15. What bothers you?
Many times, I find inspiration in what bothers me. Injustice can motivate you to speak out for those who have no voice. What stirs your spirit with righteous indignation can be a theme you tackle in your next blog, magazine article, or book.

No matter where you are or what you are doing—working, driving, sleeping, eating, playing with the kids, etc.—the key to finding inspiring ideas about which to write is this: Stay in tune with both the natural world and the spiritual world so God's perspectives show through in your prose. Whether it's a simple letter or a master work of art, the object is always to glorify God with our writing.

If you put these 15 tips into practice, you'll soon find coming up with something to write about isn't really all that difficult. We've all had experiences and feelings and revelation. These fuel our writing. The harder part is selecting a theme that will interest the readers. So let's move on to this challenge—and overcome it.

Three Strategic Tips on Selecting Themes

Now that you have an inspiration, you need a theme—something that ties your thoughts about an idea together. You could easily write about a simple or profound revelation you've received, but without nailing down a single theme your blog could turn into a run-on book with no glue to hold together the string of ideas. Even if your blog is supposed to turn into a book, your book theme will be made up of micro-themes, or chapters. Consider this time-tested wisdom on selecting themes.

1. Boil down your theme to one word.
Before you ever sit down to write, choose that word. Maybe it's *betrayal*. Maybe it's *faith*. Maybe it's *fear*. Maybe it's *freedom*. Maybe it's *leadership*. Maybe it's *overcoming*. What one word describes best the theme of what you are writing about? This exercise can help you maintain laserbeam focus during the writing process.

2. Stick with one point.
Early in my writing career, I was taught to stick with one point. News articles have one point, even if it's an overarching point. Same with teaching articles. There may be several keys in a teaching article, but the point of the article is found in the headline.

You don't need to put everything you know about a topic in one article, blog, or book. This is a mistake many amateur writers make—and make repeatedly. There's always another article, blog, or book to write. Stick with one key point.

Piling on secondary themes and unnecessary details is a common cause of the too-long article that bores readers—readers who will likely never make it to the end of your prose. When you sit down to write, the temptation is to overload the reader with information because you've gathered so much of it in preparing to write. But don't do it. Pick one major point and stick to it. Work on becoming an expert sifter—sifting through the information you've gathered and presenting the gold to your readers.

3. Know where you are going.

It helps to know where you are heading when you set out to write. With a plan and direction in mind, you will take the shortest path to your destination. When I first began writing, I sometimes started at the end of the story and worked my way back to the beginning. Sometimes the beginning was just too hard to drum up. But that was an advantage because once I got flowing I knew where I was supposed to end up. The reader doesn't just want to walk along forever. The reader wants to get somewhere and it's your job to take them there.

Chapter 2
Tools Every Christian Writer Needs

M any people ask me what tools I use in my writing process. Do I use pen and paper? Do I use special writing software? Do I read books on writing? Do I carry a notebook everywhere I go?

The answer is yes. I do all that and more.

Every successful writer has a cadre of tools at hand to inspire them, expose them to new techniques, keep up with trends in the industry, improve their craft, fellowship with other writers, and more.

You may not use all your tools every day, but they are at your disposal.

Physical Writing & Working Tools

I love software and virtual tools, but there are still some hard tools every writer should have. After all, what are you going to do if your battery dies on your voice recorder, your cell phone, or your computer? What if the materials you need to read don't yet come in digital form? I've listed a few of the most important ones here:

Moleskine notebook

I love Moleskine notebooks. Ernest Hemingway used them, as do many other writers. They are small, thin and classy. They come now in many different sizes and colors, but I like the small classic black version the best. Moleskine notebooks are a bit pricey compared to a spiral notebook, but if you need something durable, this is a go-to for writers. Of course, Moleskine notebooks are now so popular there are plenty of lower cost knockoffs—but none like the original.

'The Elements of Style' by Strunk and White

This book is indeed the definitive text and classic manual on the principles of English language. Millions have read it. Every writer needs a copy. It includes chapters like "Words and Expressions Commonly Misused" and "A Few Matters of Form."

'The Associated Press Stylebook'

If you are a news writer, this is the gold standard of style. It offers rules on grammar, spelling, punctuation, capitalization, abbreviation, and word and numeral usage.

'The Chicago Manual of Style'
The Chicago Manual of Style is available online or in hard copy. It provides recommendations on editorial style and publishing practices for the digital age. The style guide's publisher says it is the must-have reference for everyone who works with words.

Standing Desk
Sitting is the new smoking. There are many different types of standing desks on the market. From makeshift desk extenders to automatic desks that rise up and go down remotely. If you plan to spend a career writing, invest in a standing desk for your own health. (Yes, I have one!)

Laptop or Tablet
You need to be ready, willing, and able to write whenever inspiration strikes. I wrote one of my books on a tablet while waiting on the plane to take off and land, then transferred what I wrote in those short pockets to a laptop while in the air. Make the most of your time. I am not shy about telling people I prefer Apple products.

Digital Recorder
Digital recorders come in handy if you feel an urge to dictate—or interview people. There are many digital recorders at various price points. You can even use an app on your smartphone, but that's not always convenient. I use the Xoom recorder.

Extra batteries/portable charger
Whether for a recorder or your phone or laptop, you need to invest in extra batteries. Those may be AAAs or external batteries for your mobile devices. You can also get a portable iPhone external battery back.

Soft Writing Tools
Writing tools are not one size fits all. I tend to use Microsoft Word for most of my projects. That's the format in which book publishers and magazine editors require for you to file copy. But there are other tools I find helpful for various projects. Here are a few you may find helpful on your writing journey.

Logline
Logline bills itself as a screenwriting app that brings clarity to your writing. You can write in full-screen mode with high-resolution backgrounds and even choose the one that best fits the mood of your screenplay. This is a low-cost app for Mac computers you should consider if you are just getting started with screenwriting.

Final Draft
Final Draft is the world's number one screenwriting software. Nearly all film and TV writers use it. (Yes, I have a copy.) It works on Mac, Windows, iPad, and iPhone and paginates your script to entertainment

industry standards. It comes packed with 100 templates for screenplays, teleplays, and stage plays.

Grammarly

Grammarly promises to instantly fix 250 types of errors, most of which Microsoft Word can't find. The software also helps you find the right word with context-optimized synonym suggestions and works whether you are writing emails, books, blogs, social media posts, or anything else.

WriteRoom

WriteRoom is an alternative to Microsoft Word. It aims to eliminate distractions with a full-screen writing mode that helps you zero in on the words. All you see are words on the page. This minimalist presentation can help you avoid the temptation to italicize, bold, underline, and format as you go. Of course, you'll eventually have to transfer your work in WriteRoom to Microsoft Word to file with an editor.

iA Writer Pro

If you do much writing on mobile devices, iA Writer Pro provides one of the best writing experiences out there. It offers a light grey background with a monospaced font and a bright blue cursor. It comes with features like Focus Mode and Reading Time, and lets you include images, tables, texts as blocks of content, and more. It works with Apple and Android devices. You can transfer this into Microsoft Word.

Scrivener

Scrivener is a word processor/project management tool specifically designed for writers who write books or long research papers. You can add tables, bullet points, and images, and format your text however you choose. Footnotes are easy. Outlines are simple. The corkboard feature offers you a virtual index card where you can jot notes. If you want an all-in-one application specifically for writers, Scrivener is worth checking out. Again, you can transfer this into Microsoft Word later.

WordCounter

You can do a simple word count in your word processor, but WordCounter does that and more. This online editor helps you make better word choices, improve your writing style, and even check for grammar mistakes and plagiarism. This software also shows you the top 10 keywords and keyword density of an article, which is important for online writers looking to drive traffic.

Cliché Finder

Located at cliché.theinfo.org, Cliché Finder helps you find clichés that make your writing sound trite. Just cut and paste your prose into this web-based software and you'll see the clichés marked out in red for your review. Sometimes you may use clichés on purpose, but most of the time they are, well, cliché.

Capitlizemytitle.com
This site lets you choose the capitalization style that best suits your audience. Just cut and paste your headline into the box and choose one of three options: Capitalize words with four or more letters (AP style); Capitalize words with five or more letters; Do not capitalize words based on length (Chicago Manual Style).

Copyscape
Is someone plagiarizing you? Are you plagiarizing someone? This tool will help you determine who's crossing your boundaries and keep you from accidentally publishing something editors may view as copycatting.

Citebite
Citebite is a nifty tool that can save you time citing your sources. Here's how it works: Paste a chunk of text and the URL of the page where you grabbed it. Hit the "Make Citebite" button and you'll get a link that opens right to the page where you found it for future reference.
    Find it at pages.citebite.com/r6v8f6g3pvpl.

Hemingway Editor

Ernest Hemingway was a master writer, and the Hemingway Editor could help you sharpen your prose. The app signals complex, lengthy sentences and common errors. It offers color-coded highlights to help you understand where you can make improvements to format, voice, weak phrases, and so on.

Wordy

Need a second set of eyes? You can get real-time, human proofreading and copyediting any time of the day or night with Wordy. Major newspaper writers depend on Wordy. You should too if you need a fresh look at your prose.

Tip of My Tongue

Ever have a word on the tip of your tongue and you just can't remember it for the life of you? Check out Chirag's Tip of My Tongue tool at chir.ag/projects/tip-of-my-tongue. You can enter in what the word starts with, contains or ends with, word meanings, letters, etc.

Creativity Portal's Imagination Prompt

There's nothing deep about this. Just visit creativity-portal.com/prompts/imagination.prompt.reload.html and you'll get a prompt to get your juices flowing. The one that came up when I entered the URL was.

"Money is _____, and here's why…" You can hit the "next prompt" button and get another.

Dictionary
I love paper dictionaries, but online dictionaries are much faster. Two I use regularly are Dictionary.com and M-W.com.

Thesaurus
It's always good to have an old-fashioned *Roget's Thesaurus* on your desktop. But you can also use Thesaurus.com. Either way, a thesaurus is a strategic tool to expand your vocabulary. Just remember that synonyms aren't always the exact replica of a word. If you are going to use a synonym, wisdom dictates looking up the meaning of that synonym to assure the meanings are close enough to make sense to educated readers.

Encyclopedias
Britannica.com and Wikipedia.com can be good sources of information. Use the latter with a grain of salt since it's updated by average Joes and accuracy is not a given.

CoSchedule's Headline Analyzer
Billed as the number one headline analyzer online, CoSchedule's tool lets you enter your text in a box and get an instant analysis. The goal is to help you write headlines that drive Internet traffic, shares, and

search results. In my experience, these tools are helpful for newbies but less so for extremely experienced headline writers who understand what works for their audience.

Keyword Finder
If you are writing online, you should insert keywords into your headlines and body copy strategically, without stuffing. *Stuffing* means adding words for the sake of words, just to draw attention. Keywordtool.io is a good option.

The Most Dangerous Writing App
What a name for an app, right? When you land on themostdangerouswritingapp.com, you click a button that says, "Start Writing" and you've got five minutes to write as much as you can as fast as you can. Consider it a way to break writer's block.

BibleGateway.com and Biblehub.com
I use BibleGateway.com to research various translations of Scriptures, since some translations make things clearer than others or offer more modern language that folks can easier relate to. You can also find Bible commentary, which can be helpful in offering back-up from trusted sources to help you make your point, on both these sites.

Interlinear Bible

An interlinear Bible helps you study the Greek and Hebrew words. You can also use Vine's Dictionary and/or Strong's Concordance. But the interlinear Bibles online often include those elements in a one-stop shop.

Productivity Tools

When you are cranking on deadlines, you need all the help you can get to stay focused and productive. Take some time to explore these tools now so you can get familiar with the ones that are most helpful for you and start producing at higher levels, distraction-free.

StayFocusd

Are you spending too much time on frivolous websites? StayFocusd helps you drive more productivity by setting the browser to block a list of sites that waste your time for a set period so you can, well, stay focused.

Strict Workflow

Stay in the groove with this Chrome extension. When you click *Start*, it gives you 25 minutes to work with no distractions. When the time is up, click a five-minute break timer and stretch your legs, get a drink or relax a minute. Then repeat the process.

RescueTime

RescueTime promises to help you understand how you spend your time—your daily habits—so you can focus and be more productive. It runs in the background of your computing devices, tracks your time spent on applications and websites to give you an accurate picture of your day, and gives you detailed reports.

Controlled Multi-Tab Browsing

Controlled Multi-tab Browsing for the Chrome browser limits the number of tabs you can have open at any given time. This helps you save computing resources and helps you stay focused.

Evernote

Evernote is an app that promises to help you remember everything. Evernote lets you capture and share your ideas across any device. You can create project to-do lists, jot down reminders, snap a picture of a sketch, brainstorm, create timelines, get feedback, and more.

Dragon

Dragon is voice recognition software. If you prefer to dictate your writing or ideas than type, this can be especially helpful. It's faster than recording your thoughts and transcribing them later.

Antisocial and Freedom
Antisocial and Freedom block distracting sites across the web so you can focus.

Research Tools
Research is key to good writing. These tools will help you in your quest to learn and get facts straight.

Hubspot's Blog Ideas Generator
This tool has three boxes that ask you to offer three nouns. Click "Give me blog ideas" and voila—you have an idea. I used the terms Jesus, rapture, and year, and got the following results: 10 Signs You Should Invest in Jesus; 20 Myths About Year; and 14 Common Misconceptions About Rapture.

Ancestry.com
If you are writing a novel, Ancestry.com can help you explore names from history.

Google Ngram Viewer
You can see the common use of various words throughout history with this handy tool to enrich your fiction writing. Ngram Viewer searches through books—millions of them—by publication date so you can see how common words were and compare them to words and phrases used today.

Spellchecking

Microsoft Word has a spellchecker, but I discovered the spellchecker in Google Docs uses the Google search engine technology to help find the spelling of very obscure words not found in the word processing software.

Freelance Writer's Tools

LegalZoom or LegalShield

It's good to have access to legal services. I use LegalShield for document review on contracts. LegalZoom can be advantageous for filing various entities. In a world of copyright laws and contracts, at times you need an expert's view.

FreshBooks

FreshBooks is a strategic way to keep track of your freelance writing invoicing. It offers invoice software, expenses and receipt help, timing tracking, estimating software, and more.

Bidsketch

Need to create client proposals? Bidsketch can help you take the heavy lifting out of the equation. You can mix and match content, fees, and designs to create proposals quickly and even get electronic signatures.

TripIt
TripIt organizes your travel plans in one place, finds alternative flights, sends real-time alerts, helps you get the best seat, and more.

Expensify
Expensify lets you import expenses directly from a credit card to create free expense reports quickly. This is a time saver if you have a lot of expenses to track and submit to clients.

Dropbox
Dropbox is a file storage system that lets you share documents with others. Google Drive and Box are alternatives.

DocuSign
DocuSign lets you set up an electronic signature for contracts. It can be a convenient alternative, especially as fax machines go the way of the dinosaur.

Reminder Tools

There are a cadre of reminder tools that are free or paid. You can explore the features and functions of Teuxdeux, Now Do This, Reminder, Oh Don't Forget, Remember the Milk, and Better Buzzer. Other tools you may want to explore include:

Unstuck

Zen Writer
Byword
Stopwatch
Write or Die 2
ImTranslator
Toggl
TextExpander

Chapter 3
An Easy Guide to Structuring a Simple Story

Now that you've received revelation—and plowed through the spiritual battles opposing its release—where do you begin with sharing what you've learned in writing? Now that you've witnessed significant events in the Body of Christ, or noticed a news headline that caused righteous indignation in your spirit, how do you frame your views in print in a way that will capture the readers' attention?

If you want to bring readers to a logical conclusion—if you want anyone to catch your drift—it's important to understand how to structure an article or book chapter—which essentially is a much longer article—with a focus on a topic that fits into a broader theme.

If you're an avid reader, you've probably started reading articles and books you didn't finish because the headline or book cover demanded your attention, but the author could not keep you hooked all the way to the end. One of our goals as writers is to take readers on a journey that is carefully mapped out with a clear purpose. In order to do that, you need a logical structure. You need to start with words that demand attention, keep them on the hook through the twists and turns in the middle, and end with a bang so they want to read your next work.

It takes tremendous thought and effort to craft a work of writing that keeps your readers' eyeballs on your words from beginning to end in an age of short attention spans, but consider the words of Samuel Johnson, an English writer who made lasting contributions to English literature as a poet, essayist, moralist, literary critic, biographer, editor, and lexicographer who lived and died in the 1700s: "What is written without effort is in general read without pleasure." Can someone say amen?

Just like prayer is hard work, writing is hard work. But just as prayer can be enjoyable, writing can be enjoyable. When you are writing, you are not serving yourself; you are serving your reader. Make every word count. Like Enrique Jardiel Poncela, a Spanish playwright and novelist, said, "When something can be read without effort, great effort has gone into its writing." Another amen, please.

Before you sit down to write, take the time to create an outline that offers the order of the information you are presenting. There are different structures in writing, including the storytelling approach, the inverted pyramid, *The Wall Street Journal* formula, process stories, and op-eds—or editorials.

Of course, if you are feeling super creative then just start writing. But at some point, you'll need to think through the logic of your written presentation. Let's explore some of the most common writing approaches:

The Storytelling Approach

There's a storytelling approach that is just that. It tells a story. Every book, article, screenplay, or blog ultimately tells a story—but some writers do it better than others. While there are different ways to tell a story—and you have the freedom to choose your style—you need a story to tell or your readers won't read what you write—much less remember your point.

Let me say this another way for emphasis: No matter how many facts, figures, and expert insights you have, you still need to craft a story. Without a story, your writing becomes academic, like a research paper.

As you write, keep asking yourself this question: "What is the story?" Then go beyond that: "What is the lesson in the story? What is the moral of the story?" No matter what your style or topic, you need to tell a story of some kind to season your story and illustrate your point. You need what we call "color."

Build a Logical Sequence

Once you decide what your story is, you are ready to take the next step: determining the best way to tell it. Begin by considering the most logical flow or sequence of events. All stories have a beginning, middle, and an end, but not all stories start at the beginning. Your quest is to give your reader the information they need when they need to read it, keeping them engaged even as you inform, entertain, or persuade their hearts. That may mean starting from the past, present, or future.

In feature writing, some stories start in the now and fill in history for context—or even start at the end and tell the story of how someone got to where they are now. Sometimes, starting a story at the beginning is a boring approach. Sometimes it's the only approach. Sometimes you start at the middle—where someone is now—and explore how they got where they are before letting them tell you where they are going. Either way, there is still a logical sequence that results in the most powerful presentation possible.

Are you writing a news article? Start at the beginning with the "right now" facts. Writing a teaching article or blog, your logical structure is to present a problem or challenge and offer a solution. Teaching articles often start with an anecdote to illustrate the problem or challenge and offer Scriptures and spiritual insights—and sometimes even more anecdotes—to demonstrate and advise on a solution.

Inverted Pyramid Style

Newspaper reporters use the Inverted Pyramid Style, but no matter what you are writing there is truth in this model to help you. Essentially, this is the five W's and the H. These elements are offered up front, followed by supporting information and background details. If you read any standard daily newspaper, you'll find this structure. Let's explore it here:

- Who: Who is the story about?
- What: What is happening?
- When: When did it happen?
- Where: Where did it happen?
- Why: Why did it happen?
- How: How did it happen?

Every story is either about a person or an event and every story should contain these five W's and an H. Even if it's not a newspaper article, these elements will be present in almost all your article writing, though perhaps in a different expression. It's also noteworthy to understand that the order of these elements may change depending on the importance of the information being presented. In the Inverted Pyramid Style, the most important information goes up top and the less important information goes at the bottom.

The Wall Street Journal Formula

The Wall Street Journal has a classic formula for writing a feature story. This formula is actually the most common method in the industry. It's a four-step process: Beginning, Nut Graph, Body, Ending. Let's explore this model:

1. In the beginning...

This is also commonly called the lead, or lede. By Merriam-Webster's definition, a *lede* is "the introductory section of a news story that is intended to entice the reader to read the full story." Typically, the *Wall Street Journal* formula starts with an anecdote or illustration of the theme with a specific example. I offer specific examples in the study manual that accompanies this book.

2. Nut graph—or theme

Continuing with *The Wall Street Journal* formula, shortly after the beginning, the writer states the point of the article. This tells the readers where you are going to take them. It's like you are the driver of the car and you are taking them down a lovely country road. You want to give them about three sentences that tell them what to expect on the journey.

The Poynter Institute, a thought leader in journalism, offers four purposes for the nut graph: (1) It justifies the story by telling readers why they should care; (2) It provides a transition from the lead and explains the lead and its connection to the rest of the story; (3) It often tells readers why the story is timely; and (4) It often includes supporting material that helps readers see why the story is important.

Ken Wells, a writer and editor at *The Wall Street Journal*, described the nut graph as "a paragraph that says what this whole story is about and why you should read it. It's a flag to the reader, high up in the story: You can decide to proceed or not, but if you read no farther, you know what that story's about."[1]

3. Body copy

In *The Wall Street Journal* formula, the body copy is where you provide details that elaborate on the theme. Tell the reader what is happening, why and what's being done about the situation. Use facts and figures if you can find them. Use quotes from others who can help you tell facets of the story you would otherwise never know.

4. Ending with a bang

The final step in *The Wall Street Journal* formula brings closure to the reader. You can tie the end to the beginning and go full circle. You can speak to the future of what you are writing about. You can end with a powerful quote. I offer specific examples in the study manual that accompanies this book.

Process Stories

We've so far talked about chronological and narrative stories, but process stories could be the right approach for your project. A process story is one that revolves around arguments, debates, and issues. This type of article, blog, or book might offer multiple perspectives on some controversial issue, like alcohol use in the church or when the rapture is coming—or if there will even be a rapture.

Investigative reports fall into the process story category, but not all process stories are news. Some, again, explore issues and arguments. The key to successful process stories is to lay out the facts and arguments and get out of the readers' way. Don't insert your opinion unless you carry strong authority on the topic.

Opinion Pieces

While you should be cautious about inserting your opinion into news articles or other story types that are fact-based, there is a place for your opinion on current events. It's called the editorial column, or op-ed.

In an editorial, you focus on an issue or problem that stirs you. Maybe it's an injustice. Maybe it's a trend rolling through culture. Maybe it's a problem in the church. You pray and seek the Lord's heart on the matter, then open with a sentence bomb. In other words, make a bold stand right out of the gate as to what you believe about the matter. Get emotional, but stay gracious.

With an op-ed, a winning strategy is to find three main points on which to pontificate, but keep everything aligned with your bombshell opening. Use an anecdote if you can to show how the issue is impacting someone—even if it's you. Don't preach, but educate.

Remember, the idea of an op-ed is to persuade, but not to twist arms. And you want to reach people who don't necessarily agree with you rather than just preaching to the choir. That means your tone must be reasonable, not condemning. And be sure to propose a solution to the problem, or you're just complaining.

Revise, Revise, Revise

I could say the word *revise* 10 or 20 times and include it in every lesson and it still wouldn't be enough. Like Peter said, "Therefore I will not be negligent to always remind you of these things..." (2 Peter 1:12). In your revision process, you may need to delete information that isn't as necessary in order to add more relevant information. You may need to clarify your writing in certain places, or just fix grammar. Make sure you've made your point, that your audience can relate to your tone, etc.

Robert Cormier, an author and journalist known for his pessimistic novels, once said, "The beautiful part of writing is that you don't have to get it right the first time, unlike, say, a brain surgeon."

And Michael Crichton, blockbuster best-selling author of *Jurassic Park* and other titles, would tell you: "Books aren't written—they're rewritten. Including your own. It is one of the hardest things to accept, especially after the seventh rewrite hasn't quite done it."

[1] The Nut Graf, Part 1
ttps://www.poynter.org/news/nut-graf-part-i

Chapter 4
21 Building Blocks of Great Non-Fiction Books

In high school, I read plenty of literature. I've always enjoyed fiction and found George Orwell books like *1984* and *Animal Farm* fascinating, along with F. Scott Fitzgerald's *The Great Gatsby*. I fed on the non-fiction story-telling style of classics like Truman Capote's *In Cold Blood*, leadership books like Dale Carnegie's *How to Win Friends and Influence People*, and Malcolm Gladwell's *The Tipping Point*. Of course, I've read more Christian teaching books at this point in my life than anything else I read in high school or in my business-building days.

What I've learned from my diverse reading—and diverse writing—is this: No matter what your non-fiction book is about, there are building blocks that make it a success in the eyes of man and the eyes of God. Make no mistake, the eyes of God are the most important. You need His grace, His revelation, His anointing—you need His help. I believe if your book glorifies God it will reach the hands of the people who need to read it most—and that's ultimately all that matters.

Although we'd love to see every book we write sell millions of copies, the reality is most books don't. But the greater reality is if it reaches only one person and it changes their life, you have an eternal reward. When it comes to books—or any writing type for that matter—you should not write with mammon (money) in mind. We should write with God's heart for the audiences He's told us to reach in mind.

We should write with the mind of Christ (see 1 Corinthians 2:16). He knows what our readers will need before we even start to write. When we write in the Spirit, our message will resonate with their hearts. With that, here are 21 building blocks of great non-fiction books.

Before You Get Started

Your building blocks start with a few tasks that seem to have little to do with actual writing, but ultimately lay a foundation for a strong book. Whether you've written a dozen books or are just setting out on your first manuscript, consider this practical wisdom.

Gather Your Tools

We talked extensively about tools you can use to help you in Chapter 2. Now is the time to boot up, open, set up, and deploy the tools you'll need to help you write smarter, faster, and more effectively. You may only use a few of the tools on the list in Chapter 2, or you may have your own favorite tools. Equip yourself with what you need to plow through.

Create a Writing Schedule
Good intentions don't take you far unless you are intentional. If you are serious about writing, create a writing schedule and stick to it as closely as you can. I wrote my first several books on Saturday mornings between 6 a.m. and noon when my daughter was asleep or away at a friend's house. Believe me, I didn't feel like getting up before the crack of dawn on a weekend, but that was the only way I could make it work. Where there is a will, there is a way. Find the way that works for you—and stick to it.

Start with Book Summary and Chapter Outline
When you pitch a book to a publisher, this is what they will ask for: a title, a table of contents, a summary, and a chapter outline. This may seem overwhelming if you've never worked through the process—and it's a lot of work! But it's valuable in the end.

I've discovered this process forces me to think through the book's big picture before I ever start writing. While the book may evolve along the way, this summary and chapter outline—and the work you put into them—give you a roadmap that makes writing the book much faster.

Practically speaking, your chapter outline includes working chapter titles and blurbs—a nutshell of what is in each chapter. If you offer robust blurbs—several paragraphs—for each chapter in your chapter outline, you will have a running start when you sit down to write.

Chapter Headings and Subheadings
Your book chapter headings need to be strong, catchy, and describe what the chapter is about—and you need subheadings. You need to break up chapters with subheads as you chunk down the chapter into smaller themes. This helps the reader segment the breaking points in the chapter. I had a friend who wrote a book and submitted it to a publisher without subtitles in the chapters. Let's just say the publisher wasn't impressed. Subtitles help the reader process your book in chunks, offer a stopping point if they have to put the book down, and help you keep a logical flow.

Research, Research, Research
Before I ever sit down to write a book, I research as much as I possibly can. I break down the book into chapters and conduct at least preliminary research for each chapter, knowing I'll probably have to do more research as I go to clarify or expound on points I make.

By researching ahead of time, you streamline the process and your actual writing sessions are far more productive. Sure, you may wind up spending more time researching on some chapters than what you ultimately needed to compile your book. But with this research under your belt, your writing carries even more authority based on your knowledge and understanding of the topic. You can always save that research and use it for blogs to promote your book.

Back Up Your Work from the Beginning
Before you ever start writing, put a rock-solid backup system in place. I have a Time Machine for my Macintosh but I also have a synching program called iDrive that automatically backs up my writing. I learned this the hard way when my brand-new computer crashed and took my completed manuscript with it. I had to pay a data recovery service a boatload of money to retrieve it, which took weeks and was obviously stressful.

Ready, Set Go Writing!
Now that you've gathered your tools, set your writing schedule, done your research, and have your backup systems in place, it's time for the fun part. You can actually begin to write. Consider these nuggets as you begin your journey down the path to a completed blog, screenplay, manuscript, or some work of writing.

Know Your Audience
Who has God called you to reach? Who do you relate to most? Who relates to you? It's vital to understand your audience—to know your readers—before you

put pen to paper or type one single key on the keyboard. That's because you need to write in a tone that matches the reading comprehension level, knowledge level, and felt needs of the audience God is calling you to reach.

Keep in mind that audience may change depending on what God has commissioned you to write at any given time. That means your tone may change. If you are writing on prayer, your tone will be different than if you are writing on leadership. If you are writing to business leaders, by contrast, your tone and language would be much different than if you are writing to soccer moms or scientists.

Know your audience intimately. What are their challenges? What are their desires? How can you help them? Empathize with them. Understand the struggles, the hardships, the deep desires of their hearts; then write with all of that in mind by the inspiration of the Holy Spirit.

Write Your Passion
Write on topics about which you have great passion. Passion is your motivator. If you aren't passionate about your writing, it will probably take you weeks to get around to the next blog or years to complete that unfinished book. If you aren't passionate about what you are writing, why should anybody else be? If you aren't on fire for the words you are publishing, how can they fire anyone else up?

Know this: The spirit in which you write your manuscript will shine through. When you are passionate about something, that zeal, enthusiasm, and love are evident. Your book or blog will not only be filled with words on a page—those words will leap off the page to those who share your passion and ignite in others new passion for the topic about which you are writing.

Read What Has Already Been Written
Some authors or preachers want to write in a bubble, a vacuum, or a silo. They don't want to be influenced by anything anyone else has ever said or written about a topic. There can be wisdom in that approach and I respect that.

However, I find the ultimate wisdom for a writer is to feed yourself on the topic at hand and allow the Holy Spirit to help you process the information and give you new revelations. After all, Ecclesiastes 1:9 tells us plainly there is nothing new under the sun. However, the way you present the information or revelation may help someone understand in a better way.

It's my strong opinion that you need to educate yourself on the subject matter as deeply as you can before you write a book on the topic. Again, ultimately there is nothing new under the sun. Everyone has written books on every topic you can imagine. And there is an audience of people God has specifically called you to reach who want to read what you write. This audience appreciates your voice and wisdom and authority and wants to glean from your perspectives on the given topic.

Write the Book You've Always Wanted to Read
What new perspective do you bring to the table? What new angle can you offer an ancient truth? What book or blog topic is missing from the marketplace? Write the book you've always wanted to read.

In reading what others have written on a topic, you can see what hasn't been said or position yourself to release something vital in a new way that will open many eyes after your own eyes are opened. You can also quote or cite other books in your work to give credit to others who walked in a revelation before you, and to give credibility to some new perspective the Lord gives you.

Tell a Story
It's one thing to write what you know about something. It's another thing to write what you've experienced—or what others have experienced. Good writing goes beyond "telling" into "showing" through stories. *New York Times* best-selling author Malcolm Gladwell is known for telling stories that illustrate his theories, bringing them to life. Mark Batterson hit the best-sellers list with *The Circle Maker*, which centered initially on a story about Honi from the historian Josephus' chronicles. Jesus told many stories as He shared the gospel. Interview people,

draw from your experiences, or find old parables or anecdotes to bring your story to life.

Write with Authority

If you aren't an authority on a subject, you shouldn't be writing about it. So, when you write, let your confidence—not arrogance, mind you, but certainty— shine through in your writing. If you aren't confident, then read, research, and pray until you are confident. If your writing lacks authority, you will not convince, persuade, or even educate your audience. Savvy readers recognize an authoritative voice.

Avoid Dogmatism

While you want to write with authority, you need to be careful not to slip into a dogmatic attitude. A dogmatic attitude is when you express your opinions as if they were facts. It's OK to have an opinion on prayer or leadership or prophecy or business—even a strong one—but that doesn't make it Gospel truth. Ultimately, our writing should attempt to share God's heart on a matter.

Of course, we can and do have opinions, just as Paul the apostle offered his insights at times. But if we are going to offer a strong opinion in our writing we should qualify it as such. Paul wrote, "Now concerning virgins, I have no command from the Lord. Yet I will give my judgment as one who has obtained mercy from the Lord to be faithful" (see 1 Corinthians 7:25).

Rely on Facts and Figures When Needed

Facts and figures on trends, cultural issues, and matters of the church can help you show a picture of how severe—or how encouraging—current realities are. If you are writing about abortion, you should cite figures—both historical and modern—for comparison. The same goes with any issue in the news or any trend you are trying to prove. Use facts and figures liberally. Prove your case if you can and if you can't then don't write the story.

Use Scripture to Make Your Point

Facts and figures can make your writing strong, but Scripture is the end-all. Whether you are writing to a Christian audience that wants to learn about church marketing or marriage counseling or discipleship or deliverance ministry, relying on Scripture is the number one source of credibility in your manuscript. Use Scripture as much as possible, either directly or paraphrased with references, to help make your points.

Quote the Experts

Beyond facts and figures and the Bible, you can quote experts in whatever field you are writing about to honor them for their work and to help put an exclamation point on your point. I often quote other writers in my books, especially when they have a particular revelation that was pioneering in their day or when they were the ones who originally taught me the concept. It's right and biblical to give honor where honor is due (see Romans 13:7).

When You Think You're Done

When you think you're done, you're probably not done yet—at least not the first two times you think you are done. Elmore Leonard, who was an American novelist, short story writer, and screenwriter, once said, "If it sounds like writing, I rewrite it." Truman Capote, an American novelist, screenwriter, playwright, and actor, revealed, "I'm all for scissors. I believe more in the scissors than I do in the pencil." And Raymond Chandler, a detective fiction writer, quipped, "Throw up in your typewriter every morning. Clean up every noon."

Of course, there are times you don't have the liberty to make things "perfect," because deadlines loom. But you should strive for excellence and excellence is a process.

Revise, Revise, Revise
The first draft is just a draft. I do my first draft quickly, but not too quickly. I try to bring it as close to completion as possible without getting bogged down in issues like facts and figures or Scripture references that need to be validated. The second draft is to refine and add in missing info. The third draft is my final draft. You may need more drafts than that to get the manuscript where you want it to be, and any

editor at any publishing house will end up having questions on various aspects of your work no matter how much editing you do.

Get A Fresh Set of Eyes

Every writer needs a fresh set of eyes. You can ask another writer friend to take a look, or even a family member who knows nothing about writing. They may add fresh perspective, help you see where things are not clear, or just encourage you how awesome you are.

Pick a Strong Book Title and Subtitle

They say you can't judge a book by its cover, but people do judge books by the artwork and the title—and subtitle. Take a look at how popular books are titled and subtitled. Go to the bookstore. Walk up and down the aisles—all the aisles. Brainstorm. You can start your book with a working title and subtitle but always be praying and listening for something better.

Chapter 5
25 Key Elements of Strong Creative Writing

Although some writing essentials apply across the board—such as grammar, voice, style, and audience relevance—fiction writing is a different beast than news reporting or social commentary. Put another way, blogging, news reporting, and social commentary demand a level of creativity, but fiction writing—whether it's short stories, novels, television, or film—raises the inspiration bar to the next level.

In fiction writing you are not only charged with capturing the attention of your audience, you must also develop a plausible plot complete with twists, compelling characters your readers will love or hate, and endings that leave them wanting more. Indeed, fiction writing stretches your imagination to the absolute limits and then some.

I'm reminded of the words of Scottish fiction author Iain M. Banks: "The trouble with writing fiction is that it has to make sense, whereas real life doesn't."

When I was in college, I took a creative writing class. The assignment was to focus on deep descriptive elements. I wrote about my college roommate, who refused to do dishes. When I grew weary of well-doing in the kitchen, I decided to let her dishes pile up and over the edge of the sink. I waited impatiently for her to get a clue, but she feigned ignorance.

Some days later, I flew to Dallas to visit my parents for Christmas. I thought, "Surely this will force her hand to put on dishwashing gloves and grab a sponge." To my dismay, when I returned there was green fuzz growing on the pots and pans.

I had never seen green fuzz on dishes. I guess my professor hadn't either. My professor took points off my grade for an imagination that was too fantastic—only it was true. In that, I discovered Banks' statement was accurate: "The trouble with writing fiction is that it has to make sense, whereas real life doesn't." Sometimes real life is stranger than fiction and true stories are too far out for fiction readers to swallow.

Keep in mind you have five main tools in your fiction writing bag: description, action, interior dialogue, exterior dialogue, and emotion. In that context, here are 25 elements of strong creative writing.

1. Read lots of fiction.

If you want to write poems, read poems. If you want to write short stories, read short stories. If you want to write movie scripts, read movie scripts. That said, don't read only one type of fiction or you will be a one-dimensional writer. As you read, take the time to pick apart what the writer has done with characters, transitions, conflict, and other story elements. Write with a pen in your hand.

English writer Michael Moorcock said, "My first rule was given to me by T.H. White, author of *The Sword in the Stone* and other Arthurian fantasies and was: Read. Read everything you can lay hands on. I always advise people who want to write a fantasy or science fiction or romance to stop reading everything in those genres and start reading everything else from Bunyan to Byatt."

2. Capture their attention in the first sentence.

This holds true in any form of writing but if you can't capture your readers' attention in the fiction world you will lose them much faster than in the non-fiction world. Lead with the drama or strong emotion. Open with a strong conflict. Make your character think, say, or do something shocking. Come out of the gate with some sort of tension.

3. Develop dynamic characters.

You won't spend hours developing every character in your fiction work, but you should know your protagonist and antagonist inside and out. Your main characters must be three-dimensional. You have to know them so well, they are almost like your best friend—or your worst enemy.

You can glean character traits from real life people you've come in contact with over the years. You can also study psychology as you develop the inner life of your characters. This study will help you understand struggles people face that you may never understand through personal experience alone. And every character should have a flaw.

Take some time to develop character profiles, even determining details that may never come out in your story. Start by giving them a name, age, job, ethnicity, and religion. Are they single or married? Do they have children? What do they look like? Where do they live? Are they pet owners? What hobbies do they enjoy? What do they love and hate? What motivates them? What deep, dark secrets do they carry? What do they dream about or fear? Are they outgoing? Reserved? What is their favorite color, favorite foods, etc.? What are their strengths and weaknesses? Their goals in life? Who are their friends and family? Their enemies?

Write a character profile and be sure every action your character takes is in line with that profile for consistency's sake. The main elements that make up every character personality are childhood influences (largely parents), past and present relationships, career orientation, hobbies, and worldview.

Remember, your protagonist has to want something so badly they are willing to do almost anything to get it. And your protagonist must fail over and over again before getting what they want. This is part of the conflict and metamorphosis that gives every story tension.

People don't necessarily have to like your protagonist. The protagonist can be a quirky jerk. Your audience must relate to the plight of the protagonist. Your protagonist has to learn and grow through the story. The protagonist must have a life-changing epiphany at some point on the journey. Maybe they started off as a quirky jerk but are transformed into a quirky giver.

As you write, remember to show who your character is rather than tell. Fiction writing is more about showing through action than telling through long descriptive paragraphs that slow down the pace of your story.

4. Choose your point of view. Every story is narrated from a point of view.

Will you write in the first person, the second person, or the third person? The first person is the "I" or "We" perspective. The second person is the "you" perspective. The third person is the "he, she, it, they" perspective.

The first person perspective writes the story from either the protagonist or antagonist's view. They are telling the story through their own biases, which may or may not be accurate.

The second person perspective is a character telling the reader as if they are participating in the story. You see this approach in some writing—especially in movies—where a character suddenly begins speaking to the audience. The movie *Ferris Bueller's Day Off* made this popular in the 1980s.

The third person perspective is interesting because the narration could be from an outsider's view, reporting what they see with their own bias. This is called third person limited. Third person narration could be from an omniscient point of view—as if the narrator knows what is going on in every character's head. This is called third person omniscient.

Keep in mind that the narrator's voice must be consistent. For example, are they a Pollyanna or a pessimist? The narrator, then, becomes a character by default even if they are only telling the story by observation from a consistent perspective. It is possible that by the end of the story the narrator is changed by what happens in the story.

5. Make every word of dialogue count.

Dialogue is not for dialogue's sake. Every word should move the plot forward. Begin listening to how people really talk before you write dialogue. Help your readers feel the emotion by choosing the right words, emphasizing certain words in italics, adding descriptors about their eyes rolling, their hands sweating, their legs fidgeting, etc. Remember, good dialogue usually doesn't tell you exactly what the character is thinking. That's far too obvious and takes the drama—and the fun—out of reading.

6. Give your characters difficult challenges to overcome.

Your characters must suffer. This creates tension. That suffering could be internal or external, but without suffering, there is no victory.

7. Pay attention to the pacing of your story.

Avoid spending too long on some scenes and too little on others. Don't dump so much detail or dialogue on readers that they get bogged down and bored. Find the balance and rhythm. You do this in one of two ways: letting your story sit and going back to it with fresh eyes; or by getting feedback from others.

8. Your story should have running themes common to man.

These include redemption, sacrifice, forgiveness, dealing with death, finding destiny, and the like. The reader should walk away understanding the moral or the lesson of the story. If you don't start with that end in mind, you could unintentionally leave the reader without closure—and that's frustrating for the reader.

9. Write your story with a three-act structure.

Essentially, every story has a beginning, a middle, and an end. This classic structure dates back to Aristotle's *Poetics* hundreds of years before Christ was born. Most creative stories follow this model. Although a three-act structure may feel restrictive, it actually loosens creativity by giving you a framework to transition.

Act 1, of course, is the beginning. Act 1 includes some sort of inciting incident that sets the stage for the story to unfold. The inciting incident is a problem or challenge or a choice that must be made. The end of Act 1 brings a turning point that leads into Act 2.

Act 2 includes your rising action, plenty of obstacles and missteps for your main character, a midpoint, and another turning point—usually a dark night of the soul for the main character where it seems like all is lost.

Act 3 offers the ultimate climax: a resolution to the story where the protagonist overcomes the obstacles. The final act concludes with a denouement, which ties up loose ends and brings the protagonist back to normal life—whatever the new normal is. In *Romeo & Juliet*, for example, the denouement occurs when Romeo kills himself and Juliet kisses his poisoned lips, stabs herself and falls on his dead body.

10. Write compelling scenes.

Like stories, scenes follow a three-part structure: goal, conflict, disaster. Scenes are often followed up with sequels, which are made up of reaction, dilemma, and decision. That may sound too simple, but putting this into practice in a way that captivates is a challenge. Scenes and sequels move the reader through the story in a logical manner. Every single scene in a film or chapter of a fiction book needs to be strong. Keep in mind creative writing is all about emotion, so every scene needs to elicit strong emotion from the reader, whether it's empathy, an adrenaline rush, anger, joy, etc.

11. Make your settings realistic and vivid.

Your settings should add to the story's drama, but not steal the show. Don't spend so much time describing the setting that you drag the story pace down. Offer vivid details that add to the drama for your character. Are the protagonist and his friend on the run in a hill country with wide open spaces and sweltering heat? Are they in a quaint café on a clandestine assignment where nobody knows anybody? Offer details that add to rather than bog down the story, and elicit emotion or feed into the obstacles the character is trying to overcome.

12. Weed out filter words.

Sometimes called telling words, filter words are words we are tempted to add to the beginnings of sentences that reveal the main character's point of view. Those words and phrases include *suddenly, nonsense, I see, I feel, I realized, I wondered, it seemed, I thought,* etc. There are times to use filter words. You don't want to eliminate the main character's perspective, but these words and phrases are overused and can drag down the story tempo.

13. Cultivate the art of conflict.

Conflict is essential to a strong, memorable story. There are various types of conflict: inner conflict, relational conflict, situational conflict, societal conflict, and spiritual conflict. Conflict manifests in the form of a problem that needs to be solved, obstacles that must be overcome, threats that are made, and big decisions that must be navigated.

Artful conflict creates emotionally compelling challenges and obstacles that demand the protagonist dig down deep to find the courage to rise up. That deep dig forces personal growth in the character. Conflict can drive the need for either emotional or physical courage. The challenge forces the character out of their comfort zone, whatever that looks like.

Here's a word of warning: Be careful not to introduce too many conflicts or your storyline becomes unrealistic or overwhelming to the reader.

There must be one overarching conflict and lesser conflicts that tie into the big picture. Also, the conflict can't be constantly changing. There must be congruency in conflict.

14. Create plot twists.

Plot twists are what keep your reader—or viewer—on edge. In order to be plausible and effective, however, you have to stay away from the predictable and enter the unpredictable. If your plot twist is too obvious, you'll make your reader yawn. If by the same token, your plot twist is too far-fetched, you lose credibility.

Think about what would logically happen in the story, then pull a fast one on your reader with the unexpected. At the same time, you don't want an unbelievable twist that seemed to come out of nowhere and makes the audience feel duped. Drop clues through the subtle actions and dialogue of your main characters. In this way, you are planting seeds for the unexpected without revealing the twist until precisely the right moment.

15. Increase the stakes.

Increasing the stakes in your plot creates tension. One way to increase the stakes is to introduce an ultimatum or a deadline. In a relationship story, ultimatums provide the ultimate tension and drama. Deadlines can be a ticking time bomb, a flight the character needs to catch, or some other event that's devastating to miss.

16. Tap into all five senses and then some.

Tapping into the five senses while writing is good but using body language takes it to the next level. You can find body language dictionaries online. Someone shrugging their shoulders, for example, speaks of indifference. Someone furrowing their brow speaks of confusion or possibly anger. When people purse their lips, they are tense or angry. You can work this into the descriptors in the dialogue to add to the story.

17. Mix up sentence length and structure to control pace.

Short sentences hasten the pace of the story. Action scenes, for example, may use a sequence of short sentences in rapid-fire succession. Longer sentences slow the pace down. Ultra-emotional scenes may use longer sentences to draw out the experience. As the writer, you need to be aware of how your sentence structure and length is impacting the pace and intentionally control this aspect of your writing.

18. Don't overuse flashbacks.

A flashback is a scene in your book or movie that takes the audience back in time, revealing incidents that occurred before the main story started. If you are going to use a flashback, it needs to be purposeful. Watch how other writers have used flashbacks.

Finding the right way in and out of a flashback is vital to congruency. Remember, flashbacks should not be complex. They should focus on one event that's pivotal to moving the plot forward. If you use too many of them, you risk confusing your audience.

19. Introduce rich subplots into your main plot.

A subplot is a plot within a plot. A subplot is a story within a story. The subplot runs parallel to the main plot and complements the main plot. For example, your main characters have supporting characters. A subplot may chronicle the struggles of a supporting character as it impacts the main character's struggle. In other words, subplots mimic real life. If you are going through a struggle, then someone in your family grows sick, their struggle adds to your struggle.

20. Leave plenty to your readers' imaginations.

Readers like to figure things out on their own to some extent—and they like you to leave blanks for their minds to fill in. It's part of the fun to allow your reader to imagine what may have been thought, said, or done that wasn't explicitly revealed. Give your audience the liberty to imagine what they want rather than telling them every small detail and stealing their fun.

21. Don't use too many exclamation marks!!!!!!!

It's been said that using exclamation marks is like laughing at your own joke. Use them sparingly.

22. Determine the turning point.

Turning points are some of the most dramatic moments in your story. Each turning point builds to the ultimate crisis or climax of your story. Each scene can have one or more turning point, but each scene should end with a dramatic turning point that propels the story forward. The climax is the height of the conflict or drama. It's the point of no return. It's the big decision. It's the life-or-death situation. You need to put plenty of thought into your turning points because you have to build up to them logically.

23. Work to elicit emotion from your readers.

Make them laugh, cry, or get angry. Create characters that people love or hate. Add idiosyncracies to your characters to make them relatable, likable, or despicable.

24. End strong.

You can start with a bang but if you don't end with a bang you may blow your chances of audiences coming back again. Your ending should leave your audience wanting more ... hoping for a sequel ... talking about your book or movie when with their friends. Cliffhangers can lead to a sequel, but you'll have to leave certain aspects of the story unresolved. Never end your story in an unrealistic way, as it will anger your audience.

25. Revise. revise. revise.
If it sounds like writing, rewrite it.

26. Write a strong bio.
If you don't have a bio, write one now. It needs to be honest but thorough. You need to have a long version and a short version.

27. Gather endorsements.
Gather endorsements for your book from notable people. Publishers expect this. Not just any endorsement will do. You need an endorsement from someone who has some authority on the topic about which you are writing so it's credible.

28. Solicit a foreword.
Get a notable person to write the foreword of your book, if possible. You want someone whose name carries strong weight in the arena about which you are writing.

Chapter 6
18 Foundational Writing Techniques

Every seasoned writer has discovered and developed tricks of the trade. In reality, these so-called tricks aren't "tricks" at all. Rather, they are time-tested writing techniques that lay the foundation for building stories people remember.

You can't erect a skyscraper on a shaky foundation and expect it to stand the test of time. Much the same, you can't build a story that has a lasting impact without employing fundamental techniques. And every dream home, with all its bells and whistles and charm, was built on a foundation.

Remember, no one is born a writer. You may be born with a gift for writing, but you are still responsible for stewarding, nurturing, investing in, and exercising that gift. The strength of any discipline is in the fundamentals. Learning how to build a solid foundation for your story will allow you to branch out and get creative.

As you write and rewrite, consider these 18 foundational writing techniques that will help you develop as a writer:

1. Accuracy

Without accuracy, you may as well hang it up. Would you want a prophetic word that wasn't accurate? Readers don't want inaccurate information in anything they read, either. If you are quoting someone, quote them accurately. If you are citing statistics, don't use statistics that are outdated. Find the most relevant data. If you are writing in the Spirit, write with accuracy. Use the Word of God in your stories accurately. Inaccuracy is a major crack in the foundation. Nineteenth-Century American novelist Nathaniel Hawthorne once said, "Accuracy is the twin brother of honesty; inaccuracy, of dishonesty."

2. Balance and fairness

Long before Fox News's Bill O'Reilly came up with the phrase, "fair and balanced," balance and fairness were staples of journalism. They are staples f opinion pieces, blogs, and all writing. Your characters don't have to be fair and balanced in fiction, of course.

To the contrary. But if you are writing non-fiction and you neglect fairness and balance, you are doing your audience an injustice. Fairness and balance means you don't attack someone or some group in your writing. American writer, reporter, and Cold War commentator Walter Lippmann put it this way: "There can be no higher law in journalism than to tell the truth and to shame the devil."

3. Don't write with your own personal bias.

I've seen writers communicate through the lens of their personal bias, probably without realizing it. It's easy enough to do if you aren't careful. We all have biases, like it or not. But we can't even insinuate something about another person or group in our writing.

While we must be bold, we must also maintain integrity. We will reap what we sow. Canadian author Robertson Davies wrote in his novel *Tempest-Tost*: "The eye sees only what the mind is prepared to comprehend."

4. Write with God's bias.

As a Christian writer, your bias is toward God and the Word of God. Racism is not fair. Abortion is not fair. We don't give equal time in our presentation to antichrist agendas. If we acknowledge antichrist agendas in our writing, we do so to tear down that ideology. Belgian author Hugo Claus once said, "I am a person who is unhappy with things as they stand. We cannot accept the world as it is. Each day we should wake up foaming at the mouth because of the injustice of things."

5. Write about the principal, not the personality.

You will be marked as one who attacks or heresy hunts if you are constantly writing about what is wrong with people and movements. Although there is a time to name names—Paul the apostle sometimes called out names of those in error and sometimes didn't—generally speaking, it's best to write about the principles that are troublesome than the messenger who is speaking them.

6. Brevity

You could call this focusing the story. Josh Billings, an essayist and humorist, said it this way, "There's a great power in words, if you don't hitch too many of them together."

The art of chronicling is knowing what to leave out and condensing what's left. The most effective writing makes its point succinctly. Joseph Pulitzer explained, "Put it before them briefly so they will read it, clearly so they will appreciate it, picturesquely so they will remember it, and, above all, accurately so they will be guided by its light."

There are two ways writers make a little go a long way: They carefully select their material and they use words that work hard. William Strunk, Jr. explains, "Omit needless words. Vigorous writing is concise. A sentence should contain no unnecessary words, a paragraph no unnecessary sentences, for the same reason that a drawing should have no unnecessary lines and a machine no unnecessary parts."

The most effective stories make one dominant point. The writer's job is to select the point and pare away everything else. Author Mark Twain wrote, "I didn't have time to write a short letter, so I wrote a long one instead."

If you are writing a revelatory article, then choose the most powerful Scriptures and use situations or examples that best sum up the point you are trying to make.

7. Clarity

Ernest Hemingway once said, "My aim is to put down on paper what I see and what I feel in the best and simplest way." The trick to writing with clarity is to understand the subject matter you are writing about. If you can't understand it, then how can you help others understand it? This requires background reading and research. Poorly written stories are often the result of muddy thinking.

Once you understand the subject matter, then you need to organize the material in a clear way. Choose your theme and supporting materials and get writing. Short, crisp sentences and logical organization breed clarity.

Avoid excess punctuation. Too many commas confuse readers. Watch for long sentences linked by words like *and*, *but*, or *for*. Usually, long sentences can be broken into two sentences with a period in place of the connecting words.

8. Choosing words wisely

When George Eliot, the English novelist, was writing *Daniel Deronda,* she wrote this sentence: "She began to sob hysterically." Eliot's manuscript shows that she crossed off the adverb *hysterically*, realizing that the verb *sob* was strong enough to carry the meaning she intended.

Good writers make one word do the work of three. It's calling writing tight. By choosing a concrete noun—a noun that refers to an actual person, place, or thing—good writers avoid adjectives. By using action verbs that whisper, sing, or shout, writers can avoid using adverbs. Good writers make their nouns and verbs work for them.

Mark Twain once said: "The difference between the right word and almost the right word is the difference between lightning and the lightning bug."

Remember, the thesaurus is your friend. The goal is to find vivid words to describe the subject, but be sure to look up the meanings of those words. Just because it is listed as a synonym doesn't mean it has the same meaning in the context of your sentence. Sometimes synonyms can work against clarity if it's a word few people have ever heard of. That said, a thesaurus should not substitute for a growing vocabulary but should, rather, support it.

9. Don't write to impress people.

If you try to impress people with your writing, you will convolute your message. In other words, write what's on your mind and in your heart with no fear of what people will think. When you set out to impress people, you stray from your true voice and muddy your Spirit-inspired flow.

10. Write with empathy when appropriate.

Depending on the format and topic, you should employ empathy whenever possible. You want the reader to understand that you understand; that you are not judging or criticizing them. You want them to know you can relate to their situation. Empathetic writers win loyal audiences. Now, empathy is different than sympathy—and spiritual compassion is different than soulish compassion. We want to move in the Spirit and write in the Spirit, not in the soulish realm.

11. Write to influence.

No matter what genre you pursue, except for straight-up news reporting, your writing goal is to influence your reader. If you are writing fiction, you are proposing moral lessons in your prose. If you are writing for film or TV, it's much the same. We want to influence the world for Jesus. That doesn't mean always using spiritual terms. Love can be demonstrated in many ways. The best writers are influential writers.

12. Write strong headlines.

No one will read your story if you don't write a strong headline. Your headline should be concise, specific, include numbers where applicable, create a sense of urgency, relate to the reader, and use action words. Don't try to be cute and clever. Make it easy for the reader to digest what you are saying quickly.

13. Set up the reader to agree with you.

You can lay a foundation for education by asking a question to which your target audience is likely to agree, such as: "Are you praying fervently for your prodigal?" Or "Do you want to get closer to God?" The downside is this technique will not appeal to those who would answer "no." But if you are trying to reach a specific audience, such questions will hook them into your story.

14. Write in a conversational tone.

Unless you are writing an academic paper, writing in a conversational tone will win more readers. This is true for almost any style of writing, with poetry and certain styles of prose being exceptions. If you want people to relate to what you have to say, you need to say—or in this case, write it—in a way they can relate. Writing over their heads or in a terse or formal style is typically not going to appeal to most readers. Even academians enjoy a break from the dry material they have to read.

15. Season your writing with grace.

Write like you are talking to your friends. Write as if you are trying to win their minds and hearts for God. Even if you are writing to gain the attention of those who are in error or those who oppose the cross, taking a friendly approach rather than an aggressive approach sets the stage to chip away at the enemy's blinders. Colossians 4:6 tells us, "Let your speech always be with grace, seasoned with salt, that you may know how you should answer everyone."

16. Stir up some controversy when appropriate.

While you don't want to be marked as one who stirs the pot just to stir the pot—or just to gather an audience—there are times to tackle a controversial topic with grace. There are also times to stir up controversy on purpose when your audience is falling into lukewarmness or deception. This is what I often do in my column, "Watchman on the Wall."

17. Make the reader think.

It's one thing to tell the reader what you think—or tell them how you believe they should think. It's another thing altogether to provide them with solid information and ask questions that make them think.

A strategy for influential writing is to let the reader come to their own conclusion. In this way, they don't feel like you've bullied them or twisted their arm into believing something and can defend what they believe because they've thought through it on their own. You just helped by offering fodder to think on.

18. Offer a call to action.

Whether you are writing to influence, stirring up controversy, pointing out a problem that needs to be addressed, or just looking to inspire people, consider a call to action. End your article with a call to prayer, or a call to take some sort of step. Give them specific instructions on what they should do. Make suggestions of what they could do. James said, "Faith without works is dead."

Chapter 7
24 Ingredients of Strong Writing

You read weak writing—but do you recognize the weakness in your own writing? Do you see areas where you need to improve? Would you notice if your writing drags? Is your grammar so poor that it causes sentence confusion so people aren't sure what you are really saying or what you really mean? Are your sentences full of weak words? Do you do much more telling than showing?

If we want to build a loyal following—or if we want to entice someone to read from the beginning to the end of an article for that matter—we need to recognize our writing weaknesses without letting those weaknesses define who we are as writers. Like anything else in life, from perfecting your golf swing to learning a new language, understanding what you are doing wrong is the first step to getting it right.

Writing takes practice, practice, and more practice. Most people do not become writing sensations overnight any more than an Olympic athlete becomes a gold medal winner overnight.

Writing is hard work—and a writer never stops learning and growing in the craft.

Let's explore 24 ingredients of strong writing and weak writing so you can tap into the first and avoid the latter. If you can master these principles, your writing will improve by leaps and bounds.

1. Use simple words.

This may sound simple, and it is. But most writers fail to remember this truth. Use everyday language. I can't stress this enough. Newspapers write to the 10th-grade reading level. Writing needs to be relatable, not religious. No one is impressed by your large vocabulary. Sometimes an odd, oversized, rare word is the best choice and you can use it. But for the most part, the fewer the bigger words the better.

Of course, if you are writing to a target audience of scholars, rocket scientists, or business experts, you can write to a higher level of sophistication. But most people appreciate a straightforward approach. Author George Orwell said, "Never use a long word where a short one will do."

2. Write simple sentences.

Writers follow the advice of the great Russian short story writer Isaac Babel: "Not more than one idea and one image to a sentence." The Bible opens with a sentence anyone could understand. "In the beginning, God created the heaven and earth" (Genesis 1:1). There is a time to use more complex sentences, but generally speaking, simple sentences will carry you further with most audiences.

3. Start sentences with subjects and verbs.
Although the best writers mix things up for variety, most of the time you should start your sentence with who and what, then move into the how, when and why.

4. Avoid run-on sentences.
The technical definition of a run-on sentence is two or more independent clauses are improperly connected. Independent clauses could be sentences in their own right. Here's an example of a run-on sentence: I love to eat sushi I could eat it every day. There are two sentences in there. I love to eat sushi. I could eat it every day.

Run-on sentences are usually much longer in the realm of professional writing, where sentences become full paragraphs. Look for ways to break extremely long sentences into smaller sentences. John Ruskin, an art critic from the Victorian area, paints this picture: "Say all you have to say in the fewest possible words, or your reader will be sure to skip them; and in the plainest possible words or he will certainly misunderstand them."

5. Don't splice your commas.

A comma splice is a type of run-on sentence. It occurs when two independent clauses are separated by a comma. Here's an example: I love to eat sushi, I could eat it every day. Never use a comma when a period will do. Comma splices also arise when writers try to use a word like "however" or "therefore" to break up a sentence.

Here's an example: We didn't feel we had a release in the spirit, therefore, we kept on praying. This, again, is two sentences. The *therefore* is unnecessary. British novelist Jasper Fforde once said: "Ill-fitting grammar are like ill-fitting shoes. You can get used to it for a bit, but then one day your toes fall off and you can't walk to the bathroom."

6. Rework dangling modifiers.

Modifiers are descriptive words, phrases, and clauses in a sentence. Modifiers should be used in front of or behind the words they describe. Dangling modifiers are modifiers used improperly.

7. Don't end a sentence with a preposition.

Sometimes, though, you have to break this rule. Prepositions are words like *with, at, from, into, during, until, toward, upon, to, of, through,* and *over*. Typically, you don't want to end a sentence with a preposition; but at times you can break that rule. At times, though, it sounds awkward in a headline or a sentence to write in a way that a preposition doesn't come before a period. If it affects the reader's clarity or readability, break the rule. Anglican archbishop and poet Richard C. Trench put it this way: "Grammar is the logic of speech, even as logic is the grammar of reason."

8. Write solid paragraphs.
Since paragraphs are groups of sentences and sentences are groups of words, the right words and right sentences should result in solid paragraphs. But it's not always so. I've seen too many writers offering up run-on paragraphs—paragraphs that never seem to end.

A paragraph should be four or five sentences, maybe six. If you are writing for the online world, shorter paragraphs are a must. You can avoid run-on paragraphs by focusing on one idea for each segment. Your paragraphs should have an opening sentence that introduces the theme and supporting sentences that follow with examples or statistics or quotes.

Ernest Hemingway once said: "My aim is to put down on paper what I see and what I feel in the best and simplest way."

9. Write with conviction.
The point of the story must be so well documented the reader or viewer comes away convinced the writer has caught the event accurately and thoroughly. American author Kurt Vonnegut put it this way:

"Find a subject you care about and which you in your heart feel others should care about. It is this genuine caring, not your games with language, which will be the most compelling and seductive element in your style."

10. Keep a natural style.

The manner of telling about an event should be appropriate to it; the event and its description should have a close fit. So if you are writing about a sports event, you would use lingo familiar to that crowd. If you are writing about an evangelism event, you would use gospel language, etc.

Patricia Lee Gauch, who has written over 30 works of literature for children, once said: "A writer's voice is not character alone, it is not style alone; it is far more. A writer's voice line the stroke of an artist's brush—is the thumbprint of her whole person—her idea, wit, humor, passions, rhythms."

11. Showing versus telling.

This bears repeating. Paint a picture with words instead of just telling it. Simply telling the reader takes out the emotion. Showing them pulls on their soul. Show first and then tell the rest of the story.

"If you tell me, it's an essay," says author Barbara Greene. "If you show me, it's a story." "Don't say the old lady screamed," Mark Twain opined, "bring her on and let her scream." Russian playwright and short-story writer Anton Chekhov put it this way: "Don't tell me the moon is shining; show me the glint of light on broken glass."

12. Expand your vocabulary.

Just because you want to write with simple words doesn't mean you need to stunt your own vocabulary. Again, there are times to use more complex words, such as when it's the best possible word to describe what's on your mind and in your heart. As a writer, your vocabulary should always be growing. You can subscribe to *Merriam-Webster's* Word of the Day and get a new word delivered to your inbox every day. I do.

Henry Hazlitt, author of *Thinking as a Science*, wrote: "A man with a scant vocabulary will almost certainly be a weak thinker. The richer and more copious one's vocabulary and the greater one's awareness of fine distinctions and subtle nuances of meaning, the more fertile and precise is likely to be one's thinking. Knowledge of things and knowledge of the words for them grow together. If you do not know the words, you can hardly know the thing."

13. Choose the right word for the occasion.

As I touched on above, there is a right word for every occasion just like there is a right pair of shoes for every occasion. Strong writing demands taking the time to find the right word and use it at the right time in the right story. We aren't writing to show off our vocabulary skills, or we will risk going over the heads of our readers. There is power in words, and choosing the right one can make all the difference. Stephen King once said, "Any word you have to hunt for in a thesaurus is the wrong word. There are no exceptions to this rule."

14. Write with authority.

Don't use words and phrases like, "I think," "in my opinion," or "I believe." State your beliefs as truth because it is true to you. If you write with a wishy-washy tone as if you aren't absolutely convinced that what you are writing is true, your voice will lack authority and credibility.

That said, there are times to ask questions, such as: "Could it be possible...?" when exploring a concept that you're pondering or presenting information in a way that disarms those who might not listen if you made a bold, frank statement.

But generally speaking, you should be convinced of what you write about in much the same way you should be convinced a prophecy is from the Lord before you release it. If you aren't sure what you are saying is true, why should anybody else be?

15. Write with knowledge.

One way to write with authority is to write with knowledge. If you aren't knowledgeable on a topic, it will come through in your writing to anyone who is— and ultimately you aren't serving those who are not by feigning knowledge. If you don't know what you are talking about, don't write about it until you've educated yourself. Howard Nemerov, an American poet, novelist, and critic, quipped: "Write what you know. That should leave you with a lot of free time."

16. Do away with unnecessary modifiers.
Have you ever heard a speaker who constantly says, "um" while they are delivering a message? Writers make readers feel the same way with unnecessary modifiers. There's no reason to speak of a free gift. The word *gift* implies it's free. Other modifiers include *practically*, *sort of*, *actually*, *rather*, *virtually*, *pretty*, and *very*.

17. Don't overuse adverbs.
Stephen King says the following in his book, *On Writing*: "The road to hell is paved with adverbs." Don't overuse adverbs. *Adverbs* are words that describe verbs, adjectives, or other adverbs. They tell us what, when, where, how, why, and how much. These are words like: *briskly*, *happily*, *really*, *well*, *quickly*, and so on.

18. Master the art of transitions.
Even as a very young writer, my mentors called me the master of transitions. Transitions are vital. You want your story to flow from one paragraph to another, from one scene to another, from one chapter

to another with grace and ease in the reader's mind rather than having them go over an abrupt mental speed bump or sharp left turn out of nowhere that leaves dots disconnected.

If you write logically, there should be a smooth flow from one graph to the next. One graph should connect clearly to the one following it, tying ideas together while staying true to the overarching theme of the story. It's like building a house. You build one brick at a time, but all the bricks are connected with mortar until the full home comes into view.

19. Write with an active voice.

Professionals write with an active rather than a passive voice. When you write with an active voice, the subject performs an action on the main verb. With a passive voice, another agent or unknown acts on the subject.

20. Don't be redundant.

Other than articles like *a, an, the*—and, of course, pronouns, using the same word in the same sentence is clunky. There are times to do this for effect. You can also be redundant with phrases like *completely unanimous, absolutely true*, and *unknown stranger*.
Investigative journalist Ron Brackin put it this way: "A curse of being a writer is the compulsion to edit. Take the sign on my walking trail, for example. It reads, 'Watered by well water.' One of these days, no matter how hard I try to resist, I just know I'm going

to paint it out to read, 'Irrigated by well water.' If you don't get this, it's because you're not a writer."

21. Keep grammar rules in mind.

I mentioned a few of the biggies, but be careful with the overuse of capital letters, wrong punctuation apostrophes, colons, and semicolons. Invest in a grammar book and take the time to review it. American journalist and novelist Joan Didion once said, "Grammar is a piano I play by ear. All I know about grammar is its power."

22. Don't use clichés unless you do it on purpose.

Clichés are clichés for a reason and on rare occasions, they can drive home your point because there is genuinely no better way to describe a situation. However, if you are going to use a cliché, know you are doing it. Do it sparingly and intentionally.

Thomas Pinney, author of *A Short Handbook and Style Sheet*, has the following to say about clichés: "[Clichés] offer prefabricated phrasing that may be used without effort on your part. They are thus used at the expense of both individuality and precision, since you can't say just what you mean in the mechanical response of a cliché."

23. Follow George Orwell's Advice.

When writing, ask yourself George Orwell's six questions:

- What am I trying to say?
- What words will express it?
- What image or idiom will make it clearer?
- Is this image fresh enough to have an effect?
- Could I put it more shortly?
- Have I said anything that is avoidably ugly?

Chapter 8
Finding Your Voice When You Feel
Like You Have Laryngitis

Beginning writers struggle with finding their voice. Simply stated, your writing voice should sound like you. It won't necessarily sound exactly like the way you talk, but people should be able to tell that you wrote it. Your voice takes time to develop. Maybe even years. But you have to start somewhere. When you find your voice, it will be like stepping into a comfortable pair of shoes. It just flows out of you.

Developing your writing voice is vital to audience success. Indeed, developing a voice all your own is one way you develop a following. People expect not only a certain content to come from my pen, but a certain tone, style, rhythm, and wit to feed their soul and spirit.

Anybody who has a command of the language can write. Fewer develop a voice that stands out amid the noise in the world. Developing a unique voice gives readers one more reason to consume your material.

Don't just take my word for it. Consider these words from some of the greats. French artist Henri Matisse once said that "creativity takes courage.'" Writer and editor Len Cristobal explains, "For us writers, it's the courage to believe in our ways with words and the world, in our story, in our own unique voice."

And Stephen King in his book *On Writing*, explains: "You may find yourself adopting a style you find particularly exciting, and there's nothing wrong with that. When I read Ray Bradbury as a kid, I wrote like Ray Bradbury—everything green and wondrous and seen through a lens smeared with the grease of nostalgia. When I read James M. Cain, everything I wrote came out clipped and stripped and hard-boiled. When I read Lovecraft, my prose became luxurious and Byzantine. I wrote stories in my teenage years where all these styles merged, creating a kind of hilarious stew."

1. Listen to the voices of others.

Reading, reading, reading. When you read you'll be exposed to all sorts of different voices. You can compare and contrast those styles and even imitate them until your own voice begins to come through.

Although you don't want to set your heart to write exactly like someone else—you want to be a voice, not an echo—the writers whose work you read and admire will ultimately influence your voice. And you can start with some form of honorable imitation as you find your unique voice.

When you find a voice that makes you wish you could write that way—when you are almost envious of that voice—spend more time reading that author. Australian author Joanne Fedler offers this insight: "Sometimes by reading the way others write, we feel an echo in ourselves, or the flash of a lighthouse bringing us closer to our own voice."

2. Try writing different genres.

When I first began writing, I wrote everything. I wrote screenplays for movies. I wrote short stories. I wrote poetry. I wrote, wrote, and wrote some more. Writing in different genres stretches your voice because it stretches your skills and your creativity.

Writing in different genres forces you to adapt to different audiences, different styles and different purposes in writing. Science fiction writer Holly Lisle puts it this way: "Voice is borne from a lot of words and a lot of work—but not just any words or any work will do. You have to bleed a little. You have to shiver a little. You have to love a lot."

3. Explore tone.

Some writers are just more formal than others. And some readers prefer formal language. My style is more conversational, which typical readers tend to prefer. What's your tone? Pay attention and then experiment with different tones so you can expand your repertoire of writing skills. Great writers can adapt their tone to different audiences. European blogger Henri Junttila offers this encouragement: "All you can do right now is to express the voice you have. Do not wait for a-ha moments and big discoveries, because they may never come."

4. Discover true passion.
Everybody has a common theme that runs through their writing. It connects to your passion. When I wrote for the business world, my theme tended to be overcoming obstacles. When I wrote for consumer magazines, it was still the same theme: overcoming.

When I write for Christian audiences, the theme is often one of repentance and coming up higher. Seeing people overcome is one of the passions that drives me to write. Exposing error that puts people in bondage is another. Your passion will help to unlock and unleash your voice. Bestselling author James Scott Bell explains it this way: "When an author is joyous in his telling, it pulses through words."

5. Read out loud.
When I first starting writing, I would read out loud every word that I wrote before I filed the story with a client. It not only helps you catch mistakes, it also helps you hear it the way the reader hears it. Are you witty? Do you have dramatic pauses? What emotions does the writing elicit when you read it aloud? All of

these are characteristics of your voice. When you start to recognize consistent characteristics of your voice, you can cultivate and further refine them. Christian writer April Erwin advises, "Finding your voice is a process, a journey to the center of you."

6. Don't worry about failing.
Some of the stuff you write will inevitably be awful, especially in the beginning. One famous writer said the wastepaper basket is the writer's best friend. That can be true. But don't let that fear of awful writing stop you. Have faith that it will pay off if you persevere. Author and speaker Natalie Goldberg says, "If you are not afraid of the voice inside you, you will not fear the critics outside you."

7. Look for new ways to say old things.
The Preacher said, "There's nothing new under the sun" (Ecclesiastes 1:9). There's no new story either. *Moby Dick* came from Jonah's experience. *Jaws* is the same theme as *Moby Dick*. It's a man versus fish story. But there's more than one way to tell the story. Look for that new way. Children's book author Robin LaFevers encourages: "So finding our voice is about having the strength and courage to proclaim that what we have to say matters, that what we feel is relevant, that what fascinates us is worthy of fascination."

8. Write as fast as you can.

Let the stream of consciousness flow. Don't try to edit as you write. You will find your voice as you continue writing. You can always edit later. You will water down your voice if you agonize over every word. Just let it flow. You can edit later. Blogger Leo Babauta explains, "My writing voice is really the voice in my head. It's not how I talk aloud, but how I talk to myself, in the noisy cavern of my skull. I listen to myself talk, inside, and that's the voice I try to get down in writing."

9. Keep a journal.

Keeping a journal will force you to practice and will help you develop a voice. It will also serve as fodder for stories you may write one day. Of course, your private journal may need to be refined for public consumption—but the words on the page reflect the real you, at least in this season of your life. The voice of pain, the voice of joy, the voice of your emotions will speak through your journal. In your journal, in fact, you will find your real raw voice.

Fantasy writer Dave Robison once said, "Every breathing moment—awake or asleep—has layered depth and breadth and scope to your voice. It rumbles like grinding continents, burns like lightning, and whispers like a child on Santa's knee. It's authentic and powerful and it's yours."

10. Speak the language your readers can relate to.

At some level, it's not all about your voice but writing in a voice your readers can relate to. If you are charged with writing to varied audiences, you may have to adapt your voice. Indeed, mature writers use different voices to speak to different audiences without compromising who they are.

Author and screenplay writer Steven Pressfield said, "What voice does the material want? Find that. You the writer are not there to impose 'your' voice on the material. Your job is to surrender to the material—and allow it to tell you what voice it wants in order to tell itself."

11. Brand your voice.

Some writers have such a unique voice it's part of their personal brand. Stephen King is one. I have developed a branded voice over the years in the Christian market. I use a lot of alliteration, poetic rhythm, and, at times, head-on controversial confrontation. I speak to the reader in parenthetical phrases, at times, with a touch of wit or sarcasm.

Your voice will emerge naturally out of your personality and passion and can become part of your personal brand. Author Gwen Moss puts it this way: "I believe the beauty of our writing is found in our striking uniqueness; in the lines of our face, the turns and twists of our lives, and from the real-life characters we've met."

12. Shun fear; it will hinder your voice.

If you are afraid how your writing will be received, you are giving yourself laryngitis before you ever begin. Don't let fear of man stop you. Authors Thaisa Frank and Dorothy Wall once said: "Most writers struggle to unearth voice—not only because one's own voice is simply too familiar, but also because to speak from your voice means confronting your world, your dreams, and your entire life raw and unsoftened by explanations."

13. Write with rhythm.

Find your natural rhythm, then mix it up. Don't write in a monotone voice. Just as speakers inflect their voice and speak more loudly or more quietly at times, find the right rhythm for the story you are writing and let your voice show the emotion you hope to elicit in the reader. If you want to stir righteous indignation, for example, your voice will take on a different rhythm and you'll use different words than if you want to move them with compassion.

Writer Jamie Lee Wallace explains, "The true voice of a writer is the nameless fire that burns inside, turning up the heat, licking at the mind and heart until it becomes unbearable to wait even a single moment longer before putting pen to paper or fingertips to keyboard."

14. Know the rules, then be willing to break them.

As with any form of art—and writing is an art form—you need to know and master the rules before you have permission to break them. But you can and should break the rules when the story demands it. In doing so, indeed, you will develop a new aspect of your unique voice. Bestselling author Joshua Fields Millburn once said, "The shattered rules lying on my cutting room floor have shaped my writing voice more than anything else."

Know this: Your writing voice will develop and evolve over the course of your career. It will morph, mature, and otherwise move into new realms. While consistency is important at one level, don't let yourself get stuck in yesterday's voice.

Chapter 9
Overcoming Writer's Block Instead of Beating Your Head Against the Wall

Scribes are warriors. It still takes a warring spirit today to put forth God's revelation, to expound on the Word of God with nouns, verbs, adjectives, and the like. Jezebel hates the voice of God and wants to stop you before you get started. You will have enemy resistance to your godly writing. Sometimes, that takes the form of writer's block.

Indeed, getting started is the most difficult part of writing. Don't beat yourself up if you are experiencing writer's block; that only makes it worse. Stephen Leacock, a Canadian essayist, teacher, and historian, once said, "Writing is no trouble: you just jot down ideas as they occur to you. The jotting is simplicity itself—it is the occurring which is difficult."

What Causes Writer's Block?

Writer's block can manifest as the inability to come up with an idea; this is especially true for columnists with hard deadlines. It can manifest as confusion over which of your many ideas to tackle first. It can manifest at key turning points in your script, when you can't figure out what your character should do next. It can manifest as the inability to find just the right words to express what's on your mind.

American author Kurt Vonnegut once said, "Who is more to be pitied, a writer bound and gagged by policemen or one living in perfect freedom who has nothing more to say?"

In our quest to overcome writer's block, it's helpful to understand the root of the problem. When we see the root, we can pluck it out! Here are some common reasons writer's block creeps into your creative mind.

1. Perfectionism

Perfectionism will rob you of your wild dreams—and it will stymie your creative writing. If you set out to be perfect, you are putting far too much pressure on yourself. While pressure can be good for a writer and actually force you to overcome writer's block, pressure rooted in perfectionism will paralyze you.
Perfectionism can manifest as a need to have the story all figured out before you set out to write it. However, just like flowing in prophecy, God won't always give

you all the words before you open your mouth. You don't need to have the beginning, middle, and end figured out before you sit down to write—no matter what perfectionism tells you.

2. Fear

Fear is a new writer's nemesis. There's the fear of writing a bad story, the fear no one will read what you write, the fear that you'll get rejected or persecuted for what flows from your pen. There's the overarching fear of failure. Fear can manifest in many ways—and fear drives procrastination. Writer's block and procrastination are cousins. Write it afraid if you have to; just start writing!

Erica Jong, who wrote the preface to *The New Writer's Handbook 2007: A Practical Anthology of Best Advice for Your Craft and Career* put it this way: "All writing problems are psychological problems. Blocks usually stem from the fear of being judged. If you imagine the world listening, you'll never write a line. That's why privacy is so important. You should write first drafts as if they will never be shown to anyone."

3. Bad timing

Sometimes, there's just no grace on you to write in the moment. Learn to recognize the wind of God in your writing. Discern the grace to write and tap into that grace and you'll flow like a river. When the river dries up, don't try to paddle on dry ground.

4. Vain imaginations

Fear is only one of the vain imaginations that can hit your soul when you sit down to write. Professional writers call vain imaginations the "inner critic. "It's the voice that tells you you're writing is terrible. It's the voice that screams, "You have no authority to write, you are going to make a fool out of yourself," and the like. Cast down those vain imaginations (2 Corinthians 10:5).

4 Ways You'll Never Overcome Writer's Block

Before I share with you my favorite ways to overcome writer's block, let me warn you of a few methods that absolutely will not work. Not today. Not tomorrow. Not ever. Don't be deceived. Don't do these things.

1. Don't binge watch TV and movies.

OK, maybe if you are writing TV or film scripts, this will help you. Otherwise, it's most likely a massive waste of your time. You won't press through writer's block by numbing your mind. Take a break if you need to, but don't spend five hours in front of the computer screen watching Hulu when you could spend four of those hours writing the next great Christian book.

2. Don't sit there and feel sorry for yourself.

Self-pity attracts devils. Don't sit there and feel bad that you can't break through writer's block. You won't break through by feeling bad that you haven't broken through.

3. Don't wait until you feel inspired.

The enemy can bog you down with discouragement and distractions. If you wait for the perfect moment to write, you may be waiting forever. Determine to write whether or not you feel particularly inspired while recognizing, still, when there is simply no grace in the moment.

4. Don't complain about writer's block.

The more you complain about being stuck, the longer you'll stay stuck. If you keep thinking and talking about the problem, you'll remain in the problem.

24 Strategies for Overcoming Writer's Block

I don't have writer's block anymore. I haven't had writer's block in years. I believe that's because I discovered how to overcome it. Here are 24 of my strategies for abolishing writer's block:

1. Develop a ritual.

Ernest Hemingway sharpened 20 pencils before he started writing. Basketball players often have some form of ritual before they shoot a free throw. It just sets your mind toward the task at hand. For me, I get my coffee set up and I pray, asking the Lord to help me write.

2. Eliminate any and every distraction.
I am easily distracted by my surroundings, so I use a rainy noise generator and wear Mack's soft foam earplugs. I charge people not to contact me during my writing time, but also put my phone on vibrate and leave it in another room. I also avoid the temptation to check email every five minutes or go on social media.

3. Write a summary.
Try jotting down a few sentences that highlight the event. This helps to focus the mind and put it in a writing mood.

4. Change your scenery.
Sometimes you need to stop staring at your computer and go stare into the face of Jesus, or go outside and look at the birds and the trees. I tend to go sit on the beach. You can listen to some music. The idea is to get your mind off the task and go back to it with determination.

5. Excerpt
This one I do a lot. I start with any part of the story that will flow at that moment. Sometimes it takes longer to figure out the lead, but I know what the

middle is. So, I'll start there. It's like warming up the engine.

6. Go read a book.
Reading can spur your writing. The Bible is my first choice, then teaching books from great spiritual leaders.

7. Take a break.
Sometimes you just need to take a break. Go for a walk. Get your mind off it and then come back. You can pray, go read the Bible, or take a walk. I do this a lot as well. It allows you to refocus.

Short story writer Hilary Mantel said: "If you get stuck, get away from your desk. Take a walk, take a bath, go to sleep, make a pie, draw, listen to music, meditate, exercise; whatever you do, don't just stick there scowling at the problem. But don't make telephone calls or go to a party; if you do, other people's words will pour in where your lost words should be. Open a gap for them, create a space. Be patient."

8. Free flow write.
Use the mind traffic or the utter silence to your advantage. Whatever is going through your mind, just write it down in a stream of consciousness. If nothing is going through your mind, write down the frustration you feel about that silent place. The key is

just to start writing to break the pattern. Poet Strider Marcus Jones put it this way: "When words don't come easy, I make do with silence and find something in   nothing."

9. Drink some coffee.
Maybe you just need a little caffeine boost, especially if you are tired. Again, I always sit down to write with a cup of coffee. It's one of my rituals.

10. Pray
Prayer changes things. Ask God to break the writer's block. As God for grace. Ask God to help you eliminate distractions. As God to give you revelation. Ask God to give you inspiration. Ask God.

11. Outline your story.
If you are just starting out in writing, you should be outlining your story before you write anyway. As we grow in the grace, sometimes the outlining just takes place in our minds. But if you are facing writer's block, go back to the basics. List the main points and the order in which they will appear in the story. You don't have to stick with it, but it gives you a frame of reference.

12. Listen to some music.
Worship music is a powerful weapon against writer's block because it helps you enter the presence of God

and set aside distractions. But classical music always inspires me also. Find what works for you. The goal is to disrupt the distractions or to free your mind from the current thought patterns.

13. Share your ideas.
Call someone and talk to them about the story you are writing. Sometimes that will get the juices flowing.

14. Write anyway.
Don't worry if what you write is any good. Just start writing something. Maya Angelou once said: "What I try to do is write. I may write for two weeks 'the cat sat on the mat, that is that, not a rat.' And it might be just the most boring and awful stuff. But I try. When I'm writing, I write. And then it's as if the muse is convinced that I'm serious and says, 'Okay. Okay. I'll come.'"

15. Change your writing tools.
If you usually type on a computer, try freehand writing. If you normally write manually, try transcribing your thoughts on your phone. Shake it up!

16. Read inspirational quotes.
If you need some inspiration, read some inspirational quotes. You can Google "writing quotes" to let some of the greats inspire you with their wise words.

17. Bind up frustration.

Frustration is a creativity killer. Refuse to get frustrated. It just adds to the writer's block.

American novelist, essayist, and poet Barbara Kingsolver once said, "I learned to produce whether I wanted to or not. It would be easy to say oh, I have writer's block, oh, I have to wait for my muse. I don't. Chain that muse to your desk and get the job done."

18. Resist the temptation to edit while you write.

This will stymie your flow and can create obstacles for your creative mind.

19. Try some creative writing prompts.

Go back through the exercises in these lessons or go to a writing prompt generator for help. A few good writing prompt generators are: Thestoryshack.com, Languageisavirus.com/writing_prompts.php, as well as Writingfix.com.

20. Confess the Word of God.

My tongue is the pen of a ready writer (see Psalm 45:1). I am creative because the Holy Spirit dwells in me.

21. Continue your research.

At times, there's a writer's block because your mind doesn't feel it has enough backing to start flowing. Sometimes doing more research unlocks your creativity.

22. Give yourself a hard—and public—deadline.

This the kind of pressure that drives you to perform and flies in the face of perfectionism. Set a weekly column deadline or tell your followers to expect an article on some date and time. You'll have to deliver one way or another.

23. Type out all the key facts or quotes.

Many times, just getting something down on paper will help you organize your thoughts and could release the blockage. Organize your facts, quotes, and Scriptures in the sequence they would logically appear. If nothing else, this saves you time when you overcome what's trying to overcome you.

24. Eat a big bowl of organic chocolate ice cream.

If you prefer vanilla, go for it. This always works. All the time and on every occasion. OK, I am teasing—sort of.

I'll leave you with some last words from Ernest Hemingway: "The best way is always to stop when you are going good and when you know what will happen next. If you do that every day ... you will never be stuck. Always stop while you are going good and don't think about it or worry about it until you start to write the next day. That way your subconscious will work on it all the time. But if you think about it consciously or worry about it you will kill it and your brain will be tired before you start."

Chapter 10
Pitching Your Writing the Right Way

So, you've got a great story idea and Holy Ghost inspiration to write like the wind. You have discovered what you feel is the perfect platform to release the story He's placed on your heart. And you've worked up the courage to make the big pitch.

Congratulations! You are well on your way to getting published—or getting published in a new outlet you've been aiming at for years. But you've got one more barrier to overcome: winning the heart and mind of the editor. Armed with the instruction in this chapter, you can craft a pitch that will give you the best possible chance of success.

That said, many factors play into whether or not you ultimately land a spot in a publisher's lineup. It's possible to have a compelling idea and a strong presentation and never get an answer back from the editor—or receive a rejection letter. Don't let that bother you. It just means you are one step closer to walking through the door God has ordained for you. Keep knocking!

Crafting a Formal Proposal

Once you've determined your writing is fit for a publisher, take the time to craft a formal proposal before you blindly send a completed article or book for an editor's review. If you submit an entire article or book rather than a well-crafted proposal, you could blow what may have otherwise been a big win. That's because an editor can help you craft the angle of your writing to best meet the needs of her readers before you write it—if they like the idea.

If you charge ahead to write an article or book without giving the editor any chance to chime in on the idea—perhaps someone recently wrote a similar article that hasn't been published yet, for example, but the editor might be keen on a follow-up with a different perspective—you lose before you have a chance to see the rewards of publishing.

In balance, if you've already written the article or book, don't let this discourage you. Just don't send the whole article or book to the prospective publisher. Walk in patience. Write and send the proposal. Wait for the editor's feedback.

If they love your idea as is, you're ahead of the game and can revise your material once more before submitting it. If they have feedback that would give you a greater chance of getting published, you can preserve your original article, make a copy, revise based on the editor's feedback, and submit your content ahead of the deadline.

Writing a Strong Query Letter

In this magazine and newspaper world, proposals are called query letters. The purpose of a query letter is to sell the editor on your big idea. You want to convince them—without reservation—that the article you are proposing will add value to their magazine or newspaper readership. Elements of a strong query letter include:

- A personal address to the editor rather than a generic introduction. This shows you took the time to find out who you are talking to instead of sending out a blanket query to all editors;
- Basic information about your article idea, including a title of the work and the proposed word count;
- The hook or compelling angle of the article and how it serves the readership;
- A demonstration or proof you understand the market for which you are writing;
- Acknowledgment of the availability of photos or artwork if you have access to them;
- A brief—key word here is brief—bio with any relevant experience writing to the publisher's target audience; and
- A statement thanking the editor for her time and asking for any feedback.

The best query letters get to the point quickly, just like the lead of a story. Your goal is to catch the attention of the editor immediately so she will keep reading and ultimately be fascinated enough by your idea to commission you to write the story. Your query letter should not be longer than one page—that's about 500 words.

What Not to Do in a Query Letter

Some amateur writers make fatal flaws in query letters that cause editors to cringe—then trash your proposal before they even get to the bottom of your email. One of those fatal flaws is talking money up front. A query letter is not the appropriate place to discuss rates. Likewise, many publications have set rates that are not open for negotiation. If the editor accepts your idea, she will let you know the word count, the deadline, and the story rate.

Some editors may ask you what your going rate is. This is where books like *The Writer's Market* come in handy because the authors offer standard rate ranges based on publication circulation and your experience. Do your homework. Find out what the prevailing rates are. Don't sell yourself short but don't pitch at the highest end of the spectrum unless or until you are an experienced writer that has earned the right to charge top-end rates.

Inexperienced writers also sabotage themselves with editors by trying to butter them up with flattering words about how much they enjoy the magazine. It's one thing to express appreciation for an editor's work, but savvy editors know flattery when they see it. Likewise, don't tell editors your work is copyrighted, that you're shopping the story around, or that you are giving them "first dibs" on your work. Professionals don't work in this manner.

Don't Annoy the Editor

Email is the best way to reach editors in today's world. Most are too busy to take a phone call. They want to read a brief query and will surely respond if they are interested.

Be sure to include your email and phone number in your query, and don't follow up five times to see if the editor is interested.

It's appropriate to follow up once, two or three weeks after you send the email with a polite message making sure your email reached them, but no more. If the editor feels harassed, you will blow any future chances of working with them.

Writing Strong Book Proposals

Most publishing houses have author proposal forms. Your acquisitions editor will send you a standard form once they determine your idea is worthy of further review. Examples are in the study guide, which you can obtain separately.

Chapter 11
17 Insights Into Getting Published

Y ou're writing, writing, writing—maybe you've even been writing for years—but is anybody actually reading the heartfelt words you labored over for hours upon hours? Is anyone truly benefiting from your well-crafted stories, spiritual challenges, and teaching articles that you revised, revised, and revised again?

It can be frustrating to cultivate a writing gift and have no outlet to express that gift. Proverbs 13:12 rightly tells us, "hope deferred makes the heart sick." As a teacher of writing, I want to see you get to the other side of that verse … "but when the desire comes, it is a tree of life."

Although we write for the sake of obedience, in most cases, it's the Lord's will to use your writing to reach audiences that will be edified, comforted and exhorted by the words flowing from your heart by inspiration of the Spirit. Usually, that takes perseverance—a Holy Ghost tenacity to press past rejection and frustration and find the open door of favor from the Lord.

That said, you can position yourself for the open door of favor by being proactive in your efforts to publish what the Lord has put on your heart. Here are 17 insights to getting published.

1. Build your own platform.

Every publisher—whether magazines, books, or another medium, is going to ask you immediately about your platform. Do you have a blog? If not, create one. Do you have a social media following? If not, start building one. What about an email list? You need one. In an Internet age, publishers in any medium expect you to help them market what they publish to drive sales of books, clicks on their website, or visibility of their platform. The strength of your platform will entice publishers to give you a chance.

WordPress is your best option to start a blog. Find a theme that suits your style. There are many free themes. Search online for blogs that have a look and feel that appeals to you as you search for a theme that fits your personal style. You'll want to get your own unique URL from Godaddy.com or another domain provider, as well as a web host to host your blog. It's a good idea to buy your name, if possible. But you might also want to brand your blog with some theme that describes the thrust of your writing. I bought nextlevelprophetic.com many years ago, for example, and now I use it for my prophetic training page.

2. Search writers' boards.

You can find opportunities to write for magazines in online writers' boards. There are many that serve various purposes. Fabjob.com, Writersweekly.com and JournalismJobs.com are three strong venues. Be proactive in checking out these and other sites.

3. Invest in The Writer's Market book.

One of the first books I invested in as a young writer was *The Writer's Market*. A new edition comes out each year, but you only need to buy one every few years because not much changes from year to year. You can find it on Amazon.com for about $20. Here's a description from the website for the 2017 edition:

"Want to get published and paid for your writing? Let *Writer's Market 2018* guide you with thousands of publishing opportunities—including listings for book publishers, consumer and trade magazines, contests and awards, and literary agents. These listings feature contact and submission information so you can get started right away. Beyond the listings, you'll find all-new material devoted to the business and promotion of writing. Discover the secrets to writing better queries and selling more articles, tips to earn money from blogging, and how to develop a standout author brand. Plus, you'll learn how to create an effective e-mail newsletter, improve organization, and build a solid foundation for long-term writing success. This edition includes the ever-popular pay-rate chart and book publisher subject index. You'll also gain access to lists of professional writing organizations, sample query letters, and a free digital download of Writer's Yearbook, featuring the 100 Best Markets: WritersDigest.com/WritersDigest-Yearbook-17."

This same publisher offers *Guide to Literary Agents, Christian Writer's Market Guide, Novel & Short Story Writer's Market,* and *Children's Writer's & Illustrator's Market.* You may also want to check out *Jeff Herman's Guide to Book Editors, Publishers and Literary Agents.*

4. Conduct Google searches to find publishers in your niche.

Whether you are writing to a very narrow niche or a broad audience, new publications are likely forming periodically that you won't find in books or other internet lists. Do a Google search to find new opportunities with search terms like "*X* magazines." Substitute *X* for whatever is your niche, target audience or genre.

5. Do your homework.

Before you set out to work with any publisher, be sure you understand what makes their platform tick. Don't waste your time or the editor's time pitching a story or a book that is out of line with the type of content they tend to publish. That means taking the time to actually read the magazines, newspapers, blogs, scripts, books, etc., before approaching the editor.

Don't be the one who pitches a story that was just in the last issue of a magazine or on the website last week. That shows that you do not read the magazine and may disqualify you in an editor's mind from writing for it. In the book world, it demonstrates that you are not up to speed with what the publisher is producing.

Understand the tone and style of the platform, as well as the subject matter. Take note of article lengths and angles. Look at the types of experts they may quote in an article, or how many different sources they include in a written work.

6. Find relevant story ideas.

If there is a magazine or book publisher you aspire to work with, take the time to find story ideas or topics that are relevant to their DNA. Don't impose your idea on them; let their needs dictate your pitches. We talked in an earlier lesson about generating story ideas. You can also set up Google Alerts on specific topics or competing magazines to come up with a new angle on an idea that would suit your target publisher.

7. Understand deadlines.

Magazine editors work at least three months out. Book publishers tend to work at least a year out.

Don't pitch a Christmas story in December. Pitch a Christmas story in August.

8. Start with a local publication.

If you have no experience writing at all, start with a local magazine or newspaper. You'll find it's easier to get in the door and this strategy will help you build up some experience and a portfolio before trying to write for national platforms.

9. Pitch shorter ideas first.

Likewise, when working with a magazine for the first time, pitch a shorter article rather than a longer feature at first. In other words, get your foot in the door by offering the editor a low-risk chance to see that you can perform before expecting them to trust you with a major feature.

10. Take the editor's feedback to heart.

If the editor assigns you an article or writes you a rejection letter—most in today's world won't take the time to do the latter—take the feedback to heart. Don't plead your case or otherwise argue. Follow the editor's instructions on sources, interview questions if suggested, word counts, style guides, and tone. If you turn in an article or book that defies the editor's instructions and demands significant rewrites, you are blowing your chances of future engagements with the publisher.

11. Meet your deadline.

Don't just plan and set your mind to meeting your writing deadline—try to beat it without sacrificing the quality of your work. And by all means, if you are going to miss your deadline, let the editor know a few days in advance it may be a race down to the wire. If sources won't get back with you and it's holding you up, reach out.

Your editor may be able to help. Missing a deadline with no communication is a fast way to end what could have been a long-term relationship. You won't kill your chances for future work if you miss a deadline unless it's a habit. But failing to communicate could get you blackballed.

12. Submit your article with an invitation for feedback.

When you submit your book or article, always end with a line thanking them for the opportunity and asking if they have any questions or would like to see any changes. If they ask questions or want changes, have a can-do positive attitude. Don't argue your case unless there's truly something the editor is missing.

13. Decide if you want an agent.

Many writers, especially on the book end, hire an agent to help them get published. This can be helpful, but it can also work to your disadvantage. On the pro side, agents may have contacts and help you get your foot in the door where you would have no leverage.

On the con side, they can take a good chunk of your royalties and some publishers, especially on the Christian side, prefer not to work with them but to deal directly with the author.

I, personally, have never had an agent nor have I needed one. If you decide to work with an agent, choose one who understands your genre or niche. Ask them to see testimonials and a portfolio of books they've helped to get published. Talk to more than one agent. Let them compete for your business. And negotiate rates. On the flip side, you may have to submit your work to multiple agents to get a bite, as some are busier than others.

14. A word about contracts.

Every contract is different. On the newspaper and magazine side, ideally, you do not want to give up all rights. You want to retain the copyright on your articles so you can send some variation of that article to other, non-competing outlets. On the book front, you'll want to negotiate royalties. If you are a new author, you won't have much leverage on either front; but this is something to keep in mind as your platform grows.

15. Learn patience.

Patience is not only a fruit of the spirit, it's a virtue in the publishing world. From selecting agents to getting that "yes" from the publisher, it can take time to hit the mark on what a publisher needs and wants at the right time with the right voice.

16. Build relationships.
Once an editor publishes your work, seek to build a relationship. Pitch another article or book. Work the relationship. Always show gratitude.

17. Publishing house vs. co-publishing vs. self-publishing.
Should you go with a traditional publisher, pursue co-publishing, or take matters into your own hands with self-publishing? That depends on various factors. There are pros and cons to each choice—if you even have a choice.

Pros and cons of self-publishing
I have self-published nearly 10 books. The first six books I self-published because I had a message on my heart and could not find a publisher willing to take a chance on an unknown author. The "pros" of self-publishing include ultimate freedom. You control the message, you control the cover art, you control the timing of the release, and you collect the profits. The downside is you'll have to take on all the expenses associated with publishing the book yourself, from hiring editors, typesetters, and designers, to printing costs. That can be prohibitive for many authors. What's more, unless you have a large platform, self-publishing tends to be less successful. Even though traditional publishers don't invest much in marketing

your books, their ability to get the book before buyers and their email lists and social media platforms can help.

Pros and cons of traditional publishing
I have published over a dozen books with three different publishers at the time of this writing. The benefits, typically, are wider exposure. Most big publishing houses have a publicist and may arrange radio or TV interviews for you. Most publishers offer an advance against your royalties and handle all the mechanics of publishing, from editing to design to distribution. The downside is it can take a year or more to see your finished manuscript hit the market. You don't have much say over the cover art, the title, or the edits they may want to make. Royalties are only paid twice a year and most rates are low—below 10 percent unless you are a bestselling author. It's also difficult to break into the traditional publishing realm.

Pros and cons of co-publishing
I have never worked with a co-publisher, save one project with a partner who decided to use Amazon Create Space. I wasn't too involved, but I recall the experience had a number of bumps in the road. Now, there's a difference between co-publishing and vanity publishing. Vanity publishers print anything and everything and typically scam you out of your socks

and no legitimate bookstore carries these types of books.

Conversely, co-publishers are often connected with a traditional publishing arm and are more careful about the titles they choose. Still, there are pros and cons to copublishing. The advantage of copublishing, especially with a book house that has a traditional publishing arm, is that you can work your way into a traditional book deal. Some co-publishing brands use the platform like a test bed for new authors. If your co-published book does well, you'll win their hearts.

With co-publishing, you're essentially sharing the cost of publishing your book with the publisher. The risk for the publisher is in the cost. Co-publishers don't ask you to pay for editing or graphic services up front like a vanity publisher would. But they will ask you to purchase a certain number of books up front to spread the risk on their end.

If you want to learn more about publishing with Awakening Media, my imprint under the Destiny Image brand, email awakeningpub@gmail.com.

Chapter 12
Marketing Your Message

While your motive for writing is obedience to God, ideally, your message will reach its intended audience. That means you need to get the word out. But how? At some level, it depends on what you are writing. Blogs, magazine articles, books, and screenplays demand at least a slightly different approach but there are common principles that apply to every medium. We'll take a look at some principles in each major writing realm.

Marketing Blog Posts and Articles

Sometimes called article marketing, there are basic and advanced techniques proven to help you get the word out about your message. Of course, at the end of the day, if your message is not compelling it won't spread very far. You should only begin to blow the trumpet about your content when it is ready for prime time or you risk earning a reputation for half-baked revelations before you have an opportunity to build a personal brand. With that understanding, let's look at a few ways to promote your blog posts and articles.

1. Share on social networks.

A growing number of people glean their news—or find other valuable content—on social networks. Facebook and Twitter are obvious platforms, but your writing may find a place on niche social networks, such as LinkedIn groups. You can also tweet a series of small catchy phrases from your article with a link back to the source to maximize the impact. Google+ is practically dead, but it still has value in Google search engines. Post your articles there. Likewise, Pinterest is a different audience. Try pinning a photo from your article to the Pinterest site with a link to the story. You can even take a screenshot of your posted article and post that to Instagram with a link in the description box to read the entire article.

2. Submit to niche news sites.

If your article is suitable for a specialized news site, send it to the editor. Although it's still wise to query editors of traditional magazines—even major magazines with a strong online presence—some of the smaller niche sites are hungry for content and may welcome your submission. They may not pay you for your work, but it's a good way to get your name out there and build a portfolio. That's how I got started in the industry 30 years ago.

3. Send your articles via an email list.
Email marketing is still one of the most effective tools for getting a message out to people. Sending out a weekly article from your blog will help you build a following, and may help you build a list. You'll need to invest in an email program like MailChimp to build your list rather than sending these emails manually.

4. Write articles with SEO keywords.
You don't want to overuse keywords in your article in a way that makes your writing clunky for the reader, but you can get plug-ins, like All in One SEO, that help you determine relevant keywords for your blogs and online articles that will help Google and other search engines pick you up.

5. Deploy Facebook ads.
Facebook is getting more competitive for content. But you can rise above the noise by "boosting" your best articles. In other words, you can spend $10—or whatever amount you choose—to engage with more Facebook users who are likely to be interested in your article topic. This can help you gain an audience.

6. Social media influencers.
Work to build relationships with social media influencers in your writing genre by following their pages and commenting on their stories, Facebook posts, and tweets. When they notice you following

and engaging with them, they will likely follow you back and may wind up sharing your content.

7. Monitor the traffic on your articles.
Install Google Analytics on your blog or website and watch the share numbers on your articles either from your site or from social media. When you hit on an article topic that works, write a follow-up. You'll also be able to determine from this exercise what folks look to you for, where your recognized authority lies, and where you should put more emphasis in your writing.

8. Post articles to social media the right way at the right time.
Just as you want to use colorful photos in your stories that help pique the interest of your readers, it's important to translate that to social media.

Post the image from your article or blog to the page, then write a teaser and use bit.ly to create short links to save on word count and make for a cleaner presentation. Likewise, pay attention to trends on posting times. Although you can study set rules, it may be different for your audience.

9. Create a Facebook Live, Periscope or YouTube video sharing the content of your article.
Many people just don't read like they used to, but they'll watch a video with you sharing about your

article and that may cause them to follow your writing more closely.

10. Submit your article to content communities.
Especially if you are just starting out and have the time, you may get discovered—or at least get backlinks and more exposure for your content, by submitting to content communities like Blog Engege, Bizsugar, Triberr, or TribePro.

11. Repurpose your content.
Repurposing your content is the name of the game. You can write something once and use it in many different ways. We discussed the Facebook or YouTube aspects.

You can also create a podcast where you read the story, put together a Slideshare, parse your story into 20 tweetables, or make an infographic. There are many ways to repurpose the same piece of content if you have the time.

Book Marketing 101
Whether self-publishing, co-publishing, or working with a traditional publisher, most of the marketing burden for your book will fall on your shoulders. Unless you are a *New York Times* bestselling author, publishers won't put much effort into marketing your book beyond a few memes on Facebook.

With book marketing, you can apply most of the article marketing ideas in the last section to promote your finished manuscript. But there are many other tactics you can use. Here's a list of what I found is the most effective.

1. Broadcast a webinar or Facebook Live teaching.
If you have a strong Facebook following—or want to build one—you can do a small teaching or a series of teachings based on your book and make a call to action for folks to visit your site to purchase.

You can do the same thing through a webinar, though for most people Facebook Live is a simpler route, at least starting out.

2. Offer autographed copies.
Some readers treasure autographed copies. This is a value-add for many book buyers.

3. Hold a social media sharing contest.
Ask your social media followers to share a meme you create with a link to purchase your book. Create a hashtag for the promotion. Promise a free copy of the book to the one who shares the meme the most. Then follow through on your promise.

4. Build an online store into your website or blog.
You want to make your book available on as many platforms as possible, but you'll make the most profit off your book if you sell it yourself. Also, you can't

offer autographed copies, which is a selling point for some buyers, if you don't fulfill orders yourself.

5. Write a press release.
Write a press release announcing your book and distribute on free press release sites. You can Google free press release distribution sites. One of them is PR.com. This is as much for search engine purposes as anything else, and can be effective if you write the press release strategically.

6. Create an Amazon author page.
When it comes to online book sales, Amazon reigns supreme. But most authors are lost in the sea of books on the site. An Amazon author's page makes it easier for readers to discover you. You can create your page at Amazon Author Central. You can add photos, a personal bio, books, videos, blogs, and events. You can find my page at: https://www.amazon.com/Jennifer-LeClaire/e/B002BM3976

7. Enroll in the Goodreads Author Program.
According to Goodreads, "The Goodreads Author Program allows published authors to claim their profile page to promote their book and engage with readers. Once verified, your author profile will include the official Goodreads Author badge, which you can use to tell your fans to follow you on

Goodreads." Since many reviewers are on this site, it can be strategic to enroll in this program. It's free.

8. Offer a free sample chapter.
Offering a free sample chapter of your book is a good way to give readers a taste of your manuscript and leave them hungry for more. It's also a good way to capture their email address, which you can require in exchange for the free download.

From there, you create a series of automated emails that are sent to the prospect, giving them free articles and other content and asking for feedback on the book. The final email would ask them to purchase the book.

9. Create a book trailer.
You can hire a video pro to create a simple trailer for your book or create one yourself using a program like Animoto, which is easy enough for anyone to use and free. Book trailers can help hook readers into your book's theme and message.

10. Develop social media ambassadors.
If you create a following as an author, you can develop social media ambassadors who will help you get the word out about your new book, building excitement along the way. It takes time to develop these ambassadors, but you should keep this in mind as you put together your book marketing plan.

Marketing Your Screenplay

When it comes to scripts and screenplays, it's an entirely different world. In most cases, getting an agent is your best bet. Like editors, you'll want to approach agents via email with a query that follows the same basic guidelines we discussed in the earlier lesson. Never send your screenplay unsolicited.

Barring favor with an agent, your best move is to enter the various screenplay contests and try to get noticed. A third option is to go to writers' conferences, film festivals, and pitch fests and work to make connections the old-fashioned way.

ABOUT JENNIFER LECLAIRE

Jennifer LeClaire is an internationally recognized author, apostolic-prophetic voice to her generation, and conference speaker. She carries a reforming voice that inspires and challenges believers to pursue intimacy with God, cultivate their spiritual gifts and walk in the fullness of what God has called them to do. Jennifer is contending for awakening in the nations through intercession and spiritual warfare, strong apostolic preaching and practical prophetic teaching that equips the saints for the work of the ministry.

Jennifer is senior leader of Awakening House of Prayer in Fort Lauderdale, FL, founder of the Ignite Network and founder of the Awakening Blaze prayer movement.

Jennifer formerly served as the first-ever editor of *Charisma* magazine. Her work also appeared in a Charisma House book entitled Understanding the Five-Fold Ministry which offers a biblical study to uncover the true purpose for the fivefold ministry and The Spiritual Warfare Bible, which is designed to help you use the Bible to access the power of the Holy Spirit against demonic strongholds and activity. Some of Jennifer's work is also archived in the Flower Pentecostal Heritage Museum.

Jennifer is a prolific author who has written over 25 books, including The Heart of the Prophetic, A Prophet's Heart, Fervent Faith, Did the Spirit of

God Say That? 27 Keys to Judging Prophecy, Breakthrough!, and Doubtless: Faith that Overcomes the World. Some of her materials have been translated into Spanish and Korean.

Jennifer's other titles include: The Spiritual Warrior's Guide to Defeating Jezebel; Developing Faith for the Working of Miracles; The Making of a Prophet; Mornings With the Holy Spirit: Listening Daily to the Still Small Voice of God and The Next Great Move of God: An Appeal to Heaven for Spiritual Awakening.

Beyond her frequent appearances on the Elijah List, Jennifer writes one of Charisma's most popular prophetic columns, The Plumb Line, and frequently contributes to Charisma's Prophetic Insight newsletter. Her media ministry includes her website; 500,000 followers on Facebook, Twitter and YouTube, Jennifer has been interviewed on numerous media outlets including USA Today, BBC, CBN, The Alan Colmes Show, Bill Martinez Live, Babbie's House, Atlanta Live and Sid Roth's It's Supernatural, as well as serving as an analyst for Rolling Thunder Productions on a Duck Dynasty special presentation.

Jennifer also sits on the media advisory board of the Hispanic Israel Leadership Coalition.

Jennifer is affiliated with:

- Network Ekklessia International, an apostolic network founded by Dutch Sheets;
- Forerunner Ministries, founded by Ken Malone;

- Bill Hamon's Christian International Network;
- Chuck Pierce's apostolic network
- USCAL, the United States Coalition of Apostolic Leaders;
- The International Society of Deliverance Ministers

Jennifer has a powerful testimony of God's power to set the captives free and claim beauty for ashes. She shares her story with women who need to understand the love and grace of God in a lost and dying world. You can also learn more about Jennifer in this broadcast on Sid Roth's It's Supernatural.

Other Books By Jennifer LeClaire

Angels on Assignment Again
Releasing the Angels of Abundant Harvest
The Heart of the Prophetic
A Prophet's Heart
The Making of a Prophet
The Spiritual Warrior's Guide to Defeating Jezebel
Did the Spirit of God Say That?
Satan's Deadly Trio
Jezebel's Puppets
The Spiritual Warfare Battle Plan
Waging Prophetic Warfare
Dream Wild!
Faith Magnified
Fervent Faith

Breakthrough!
Mornings With the Holy Spirit
Evenings With the Holy Spirit
Revival Hubs Rising
The Next Great Move of God
Developing Faith for the Working of Miracles

You can download Jennifer's mobile apps by searching for "Jennifer LeClaire" in your app store and find Jennifer's podcasts on iTunes.

GET EUIPPED

SchooloftheSpirit.tv offers equipping in writing, publishing, and spiritual topics such as the prophetic, prayer, spiritual warfare and more.

NEED MEDIA COACHING?

Want more info on media coaching or training? Visit www.schoolofmedia.tv.

GET IGNITED! JOIN THE IGNITE NETWORK

I believe in prophetic ministry with every fiber of my being, but we all know the prophetic movement has seen its successes and failures. With an end times army of prophets and prophetic people rising up according to Joel 2:28 and Acts 2:17-20, it's more important than ever that we equip the saints for the work of prophetic ministry. Ignite is a prophetic network birthed out of an encounter with the Lord that set a fire in my hearts to raise up a generation of prophets and prophetic people who flow accurately, operate in integrity, and pursue God passionately.

You can learn more at http://www.ignitenow.org/.

AWAKENING BLAZE PRAYER MOVEMENT

The Awakening Blaze mission in any city is to draw a diverse group of intercessors who have one thing in common: to contend for the Lord's will in its city, state and nation.

The vision of Awakening Blaze prayer spokes is to unite intercessors in cities across the nations of the earth to cooperate with the Spirit of God to see the second half of 2 Chronicles 7:14—"If My people, who are called by My name, will humble themselves and pray, and seek My face and turn from their wicked ways, then I will hear from heaven, and will forgive their sin and will heal their land"—come to pass.

For many years, intercessors have been repenting, praying, and seeking God for strategies. Awakening Blaze intercessors will press into see the land healed, souls saved, churches established, ministries launched, and other Spirit-driven initiatives. Blaze intercessors will help undergird other ministries in their city, partnering with them in prayer where intercession may be lacking. Although Awakening Blaze prayer spokes are not being planted to birth churches, it is possible that churches could spring up from these intercessory prayer cells if the Lord wills. You can find out more about this prayer movement at http://www.awakeningblaze.com/.

AWAKENING HOUSE CHURCH MOVEMENT

We long to see the miracles, signs and wonders we read about in the Book of Acts. But many church models don't make room for Spirit-led worship, intimate discipleship or body ministry—which gives all members a chance to exercise their gift as the Holy Ghost wills. While we believe in traditional churches—and operate one—we also believe there is a deep hunger and desperate need for house churches to rise up in this hour. The Lord has put it on Jennifer's heart to facilitate a house church movement where all things are done decently and in order (1 Corinthians 14:40). You can find more at http://www.awakeninghouse.com.

CPSIA information can be obtained
at www.ICGtesting.com
Printed in the USA
BVHW071449221119
564530BV00007B/388/P